A Fresh Start
for Your
Friendships

A Fresh Start
for Your
Friendships

Ray and Anne Ortlund

SERVANT PUBLICATIONS
ANN ARBOR, MICHIGAN

Vine Books is an imprint of Servant Publications especially designed to serve
evangelical Christians.

Published by Servant Publications
P.O. Box 8617
Ann Arbor, Michigan 48107

Cover Design by Alan Furst, Inc., Minneapolis, Minn.

01 02 03 04 10 9 8 7 6 5 4 3 2 1

Printed in the United States of America

ISBN 1-56955-256-8

Library of Congress-in-Publication Data

Ortlund, Raymond C.
    A fresh start for your friendships : how to strengthen your relational
muscles / Ray and Anne Ortlund.
    Anne Ortlund.
        p. cm.
    Includes bibliographical references (p.).
    ISBN 1-56955-256-8 (alk. paper)
        1. Friendship—Religious aspects—Christianity. I. Ortlund, Anne. II. Title.

BV4647.F7 .078 2001
241'.6762—dc21

                                                                    2001033860

Dedicated
to Peggy on earth
and Jim in heaven.
Friends forever

Contents

Part II: How to Strengthen Your Relational Muscles

Portrait of a Friend II

Part I

A Fresh Start
for Your
Friendships

Portrait of a Friend I

When things don't come out right, he comes
　　right in.
When none of your dreams come true, he is.
He never looks for your money except when
　　you've lost it.
He never gets in your way except to clear it
　　for you.
He's in your corner when you're cornered.
He turns up when you get turned down.
He raps your critics when they're wrong and
　　takes the rap for you when they're right.
You can do anything you want to with his
　　friendship except buy it or sell it.
*He makes you realize that having a real
　　friend is almost like having an extra life.*

1
THE "I-THOU" NEED

There you are.

Come pull up a chair.

Want some coffee?

What's new? What's up?

Where ya been? How ya feeling?

People everywhere would love to hear words like these. People are on the hunt for togetherness, coziness, belonging. They make long treks trying to satisfy their need to be wanted, looked for, appreciated. The happy hours at the bars get packed; the matchmaking bureaus get rich.

Tie even the sweet possibility of warm togetherness into ads, and you can sell potato chips, hair removal, fertilizer, hair growth—anything!

2

GOD'S PERSONALIZED GIFTS: YOUR FRIENDS

One of God's most precious gifts to you is the presence in your life of other Christians.

Have you realized that?

The two of us lived three months in a country that puts to death any of their nationals who become known to be believers. By prearrangement we secretly met one, a single fellow in his late twenties whom Christ had clearly saved. We met at midnight, eating dinner in near darkness on the floor (his style), in the home of a nonnational third party who interpreted. For him it was a rare, cherished hour! We told him about baptism and communion; he'd never heard of either one, and he was thrilled. He told us his dream: to reproduce himself with one other national Christian before they got him.

We never heard of him again.

In this world more believers are all alone than we think. They're in jails, hospitals, convalescent homes, prisons or hospices ... or, like that fellow in the darkness, they are alone with their faith in areas of the world where there are no other believers.

If you live in a country where there are many Christians and you can choose your friends and interact with them freely, get on your knees and thank God! Only His grace has put you where you are and not somewhere else.

Why has God so favored you? His decisions are mysteries; we can't answer that. But His strategy through the centuries has often been to scatter His children like seeds over the earth, and the gathering time may not come until heaven. Oh, the response of us who are blessed to live with pre-heaven "gatherings" must be gratitude, gratitude!

Talk about a gift—the presence of like-minded people around you apparently even encourages your good health. People who have even just a few friends actually tend to have fewer colds, flu, maybe even heart disease. University of Michigan researchers have found that people with strong relational ties live considerably longer than those without them.*

A few years ago we visited a village in the heart of Africa that was almost Stone-Age pagan. We were able to wander around in it for quite a while before the village witch doctor chased us off with a stick. (He looked intimidating: he was dressed in one peanut shell hanging from a piece of string around his waist and an old felt hat. We got out.)

That village had one Christian in it, a man who had once had contact with some missionaries and believed in Jesus Christ. But his aloneness, and the pressure of the entire village against him, had driven him crazy. He had literally lost his mind. Nevertheless he is our brother, and we will see him in heaven, freed from his sufferings and honored in a white robe like the other martyrs of Revelation 7.

Think about godly Job.

When God took away all his wealth, and then took away all ten of his children, Job's response was this: "The Lord gave and the Lord has taken away. May the name of the Lord be praised."

Incredible.

And then when God took away his health and gave him

---

*Les and Leslie Parrott, *A Good Friend* (Ann Arbor, Mich.: Servant, 1998), 19-21.

painful boils from head to toe, Job asked, "Shall we accept good from God, and not trouble?"

Awesome.

But when God took away all his relationships except a crabby wife, Job screamed and howled and wept for thirty-five chapters!

Oh, carefully cherish, tend to, and maintain each of the friendships God has given you!

"Do not forsake your friend and the friend of your father" (Proverbs 27:18).
"He who walks with the wise grows wise" (Proverbs 13:20).
"As iron sharpens iron, so one man sharpens another" (Proverbs 27:17).

We Christian Westerners are surfeited with Christian friends the way we're surfeited with food.

And what do we do with all our abundance of things to eat? Many of us get picky. We criticize it. We suspect it. We choose this and reject that—"foods which God created to be received with thanksgiving" (1 Timothy 4:3).

We're ungrateful for food—we're ungrateful for friends, too. Many of us judge. We criticize. We suspect. We try to reshape them to our liking. We compete with them or dominate them or envy them or reject them—

— these amazing people around us who are living, eternal miracles in Christ;
— these amazing people around us who, sharing life with us in Christ's Body, are bone of our bone and flesh of our flesh;

— these amazing people around us whose outsides may-have warts and scars, like the badger-skin-covered Old Testament tabernacle, but who also have inside the unseen, dazzling Shekinah Glory of God's very own presence;

— these amazing people around us whom God Himself has handpicked to place in our lives for the purpose of our mutual benefit.

Shakespeare's Hamlet said of friends, "Grapple them to thy soul with hoops of steel!"

It's time for a fresh look at your great good fortune: the friends in your life.

It's time for a fresh start in learning how to handle them—how to reclaim them, conserve them, enhance them—how to *love* them. Break through all the barriers. Ask God for courage.

It's time to learn how to strengthen your relational muscles.

For years every summer our family vacationed at Cape Cod, and we always ate at least one meal at a little waterfront café called Cap'n Higgins' Spit 'n' Chatter Club. The name did it all.

Last summer the two of us returned, full of nostalgia and anticipation—and there it was: Cap'n Higgins' Restaurant.

Restaurant? Are you kidding?!

Restaurant. What a letdown. What a bummer.

3

THE SOURCE OF IT ALL

Why are people on the prowl from bar to bar? Why all their signing up at matrimonial agencies to connect with somebody? Because God has made us in His own likeness, and God Himself is passionately relational.

God wants you and me, all of us, for His own friends!

Eighteen times in the Bible God repeats, "You are My people, and I am your God." He is the ultimate people-lover! And He climaxes His whole Book with this thrilling prediction of the last days: "Now the dwelling place of God is with men, and he will live with them. They will be his people, and God himself will be with them and be their God" (Revelation 21:3).

The Christmas coming of Jesus was a huge preliminary step in that direction: "They will call him Immanuel—which means, 'God with us'" (Matthew 1:23).

"With-ness"! Togetherness! It's wonderful.

Last Monday we got Al and Margaret from the airport. They were coming back into town and we took them to their home, which is near ours; Al and Margaret are roughly our age. They dumped their suitcases and we went out together for barbecued ribs, baked beans, corn on the cob, and slaw. We talked about the Lord, their kids, business, the Lord, furniture making, a certain pill, the Lord, our kids, food, and the Lord. It's a foursome relationship that's been building for the last fifteen years, with no end in sight.

Tuesday night we went out with David and Elizabeth, in their thirties, who've been in our small groups; they're leaving soon to

be missionaries. We ate German stuffed cabbage rolls and potato pancakes and calorie-loaded cheese blintzes—with diet
cokes to ease our consciences—and we talked about the Lord,
their kids, the Lord, money raising, mailing lists, the Lord, children's ministry (David's love), packing, where to get boxes, and
the Lord. We've known and loved David and Elizabeth for maybe
eight years.

Saturday we'll go to dinner with our new neighbors who
aren't yet believers, and we may talk about everything but the
Lord! His speech will be full of words that ought to be edited out.
But they're dear, friendly people who love to laugh. We'll have a
good time and watch for open doors. They have no idea we've
been praying for them together by name every night for months.

The Source of all this, God Himself, isn't even a loner, but
three within One—Father, Son, and Spirit—in loving harmony. In
the beginning He said, "Let *us* make man in *our* image, in *our*
likeness" (Genesis 1:26, italics ours).

Then when He created the man He said right away, "It is not
good for the man to be alone" (Genesis 2:18), and He created
Eve from one of Adam's ribs—

> Not out of his head to rule over him;
> not out of his feet to be trampled on by him;
> but out of his side to be equal with him,
> > under his arm to be protected,
> > and near his heart to be loved.*

*Matthew Henry Bible Commentary.

He made them relational, and then He gave them to each other. What perfect gifts!

How do you become a friend? We're still learning, but let us tell you the basis of the whole thing with an analogy.

You may have visited a dairy.

A familiar sight in probably any dairy is a long conveyor belt of empty milk cartons, all printed up but empty and waiting. Then, bang!—they're mechanically attached from above, and suddenly milk gushes into a batch of them. And whoosh—they're folded and sealed, and off they go.

The cartons at first were all empty, and in themselves they couldn't do anything about it. They couldn't fill themselves; they couldn't fill each other. They just all had to wait to be filled from above.

You're a Christian, and you're feeling the need for friends. You want loving, comfortable, supportive, faithful, fun comrades—at least one, maybe several. You're "printed up" and looking good, but empty and waiting.

Or you're concerned about your friendless son in Houston, or your widowed and lonely aunt in Boston. We can't fill others, no matter how dear to us they are! We're as empty as those milk cartons; from our own resources we simply can't meet others' needs. Individually we must each receive from God. "Every good and perfect gift is from above" (James 1:17).

From God comes the forgiveness of our sins, through the cross of Jesus Christ.

From Him comes every gift of the Spirit and every fruit of the Spirit.

From Him comes every person's intricate network of contacts with other people.

From Him comes every person's ability to be a friend, to make friends, and to keep friends.

Everything—everything is from God.

"From him and through him and to him are all things. To him be the glory forever! Amen" (Romans 11:36).

Maybe we're combining the sublime with the ridiculous, but remember those milk cartons!

Just as you can't fill yourself or someone else with love (because "love comes from God," 1 John 4:7), so you can't fill yourself or someone else with all the capacities and skills needed to make and keep good friendships.

You can't grit your teeth and try really hard and make your marriage partner become the romantic, fun, faithful "best friend" your heart desires.

And you can't grit your teeth and try really hard and make your roommate or some other potential "best friend" everything loyal and loving you want them to be.

But God is above, and He is waiting and eager to fill that other person and fill you. This is His great desire for you both: "That you may be filled to the measure of all the fullness of God" (Ephesians 3:19)—

Full of His love!

Full of His joy!

Full of His peace!

Full of His patience!

Full of His kindness!

Full of His goodness!

Full of His faithfulness!

Full of His gentleness!

Full of His self-control! (Galatians 5:22,23)

These are the qualities that will make you a true friend, and these are the qualities that will make others true friends for you.

But you and each of them must go to God first, only, always. He is the one and only dispenser.

It all starts and ends with Him.

4

OUR MARRIAGE: THE FORMING OF A FRIENDSHIP

When the two of us fell in love, became engaged and got married, we naively thought we were compatible! We were both from middle-class, strongly Christian homes, had brothers and sisters, were in the same stratum of education, and were the same age—and most importantly, our life goals were identical, to follow God's will wherever it led us, hopefully to some mission field. Furthermore, both our families and everyone else around us approved of our marriage.

So we lived happily ever after, right? Wrong.

Even on our honeymoon we discovered the usual incompatibilities—one a morning person, the other a night owl; one hot, the other cold....

The coming together of two people into marriage doesn't solve problems, it creates its own new problems. Here are two basically selfish human beings suddenly thrown into one unit. And neither knows the other's family history and experiences, so she expects him to behave like her dad, and he expects her to behave like his mom. But he didn't grow up with her dad; how could he copy him? And she didn't grow up with his mom; how could she copy her?

[Ray writing] *Anne was a daughter of an army general, and her mother was definitely the general's lady. She was lady all the way! Imagine this: her mother never allowed any print on the table—no cereal boxes, no ketchup bottles, everything had to be in containers, and passed when you said "please."*

I was raised in an equally devout home, but, man, in our

family if you didn't grab it it was gone! We were five noisy, happy kids, and we could all punch each other and belch with the best of 'em.

[Anne writing] In one of our first months of marriage we were frolicking in the park. Ray had never had a bride before but he figured you treated one like a brother, so he got me down on my back and started stuffing grass in my mouth. My father had never stuffed grass in my mouth! I slapped his face. We were not off to a good start!

Then the seasons changed, and one night as we climbed into bed Ray reached out the window and got some snow and put it down the back of my elegant trousseau nightgown. He was so surprised when I started to cry; his brothers wouldn't have cried.... We were saying "I love you" to each other in different languages, and because we hadn't yet learned the other's language, we constantly misunderstood each other.

Different expectations! In college my father had been on the debate team, and at our dinner table he'd assign a topic to my brother and me, and we'd take sides and for three minutes apiece oppose each other. It was absolutely impersonal; we didn't necessarily even believe our positions; it was to teach us logic and it was great fun.

So here were Ray and I at our dinner table, and he'd make some statement or other. I'd take the opposite side and get ready for an exhilarating debate. But Ray, the youngest of five, could remember all those bigger siblings putting him down, and he thought I was attacking him personally. His reaction would bring out the worst in me, and we were into an argument.

There are many Vietnamese in Orange County where we live.

Some have taken jobs where they mingle with English-speaking people daily, and in a few years they can give and take in fluent conversation. But others stay at home or get jobs working with fellow Vietnamese and they hardly learn English at all.

Married couples must stay close to each other and listen carefully to each other's languages, to "get it." It will be many years before they've caught on to some of the subtle nuances and begin to understand where the other's coming from. And even if they remain close and listen hard, they'll never get it all—which calls for constant grace, and continually relaxing and giving the other the benefit of the doubt.

Paul Tournier told of a wife who was in love with spiritual things, and she eagerly communicated her thoughts to her husband. He was a good, down-to-earth kind of guy who expressed his love to her by fixing her kitchen and furniture. She was bugged. She wanted him to respond in her kind of language, and she wouldn't listen when he responded to her in his own.

At best, two married people under one roof are beloved strangers. What will make it all good?

Jesus Christ is our peace, says Ephesians 2:14: "He himself is our peace, who has made the two one and has destroyed the barrier, the dividing wall of hostility."*

We belong to each other because of our separate unions with the Lord Jesus.

A married Christian must no longer seek his own solutions, his own justification, his own rights. He must know that everything he is and has comes, moment by moment, from Christ. In himself he's guilty, but he's not condemned; Christ has justified

---

*This statement is said in the context of the division between Jews and Gentiles, but surely it's also true between marriage partners.

him. And all his hungers for a godly life and the meeting of all his needs can come not from his spouse but from Christ. He must live totally "unto the Lord," one-on-one.

And so must his partner. So the two come together understanding more and more, as they grow, that without Christ they'd never get their hearts together—there's too much ego—but He stands between them, and so they live in peace and they love each other.

> [God] will keep in perfect peace
> him whose mind is steadfast,
>   because he trusts in [him].
>
> ISAIAH 26:3

Separately they have heart-peace in God, and so they don't flare up in anger very quickly; they're not easily irritated.

Their separate opinions and convictions about how to keep peace and how to love each other would never be good enough. But *He* is their peace, and *He* is love, and *He* is the One who continually teaches each of them from His Word.

Notice the next phrase in Ephesians 2:14, 15: "He Himself ... has destroyed ... the dividing wall of hostility, by abolishing in his flesh the law with its commandments and regulations."

"The law" says "you must"; and the law of any marriage (with all its "commandments and regulations") says, "You must meet my expectations. You must be the kind of partner I picture you as being."

Even in our forties the two of us, pretty much happily married, weren't yet best friends. We still each felt under the law of the other, and we each carried a secret anxiety that we were loved by the other but not totally approved of. We each felt "inspected and graded," and each of us supposed we got about a "C."

(Some wife once said, "My husband seems like a mysterious island that I'm always encircling without ever finding a place to land.")

We never expressed this to each other, and we were courteous and went through all the right motions, but....

[Ray writing] *One evening I came home exhausted from a long day and needing comfort. Anne at her desk gave me a quick "Oh, hi," and went on with her writing. She seemed so self-contained, so complete without me.*

When we climbed into bed I asked, "Anne, if I didn't come home some night, would you notice?"

[Anne writing] I cried! I cried buckets—and Ray loved it! He needed to see me needy! I expressed my great, great need for him, and how incomplete I would be without him.

[Ray] *That encounter turned into a Summit Meeting. I told her we seemed like two railroad tracks: going toward the same goal of serving the Lord, but not touching enough. I told her how lonely I was. She said she hadn't realized how insensitive she'd been—that she thought she was fulfilling my expectations just by being Mrs. Efficient C.E.O. of the Home. We both realized we hadn't examined deeply enough each other's expectations.*

That evening we reshaped our schedules to spend more time together. Anne postponed or canceled speaking at some of her women's conferences. We set aside Tuesdays as a day to study together.

[Anne] It was the beginning of our becoming psychologically

one. We both realized we really were crazy about each other and that our insecurities were unfounded and silly. We began expressing our admiration and love more often each day, and petting and hugging and checking up on each other's feelings. Often now we ask, "How's your heart?"

[Ray] *These days for us are glorious. We laugh together more than we ever have. We work together every day; we actually switched (after thirty-one years) from pastoring to full-time conference-speaking together. And we play together and pray together and write books together and love being together with other friends or with family....*

We can't imagine delighting in each other more. At last we're truly best friends.

Don't forget—if mamma ain't happy, ain't nobody happy.

5
SOME ORTLUND FRIENDS

Well, there were Rick and Flossie. They were New Yorkers: Rick was a boxer and a dancer; Flossie did hair. Sometimes they came to visit our first little church in Lancaster County, Pennsylvania; they were related to a couple of our members. Our church was in Mennonite and Amish country, and we were all pretty conservative.

In would flounce Rick and Flossie, wearing racy clothes in hot colors. Rick had slicked-back black hair, big shoulders, and a flat stomach. Flossie had a tiny waist, too, and fluffy orange hair.

Boy, did those two love Jesus! Their out-and-out, uninhibited talk about the Lord became the talk of our little village.

One time Rick told the two of us with great enthusiasm about a recent match he'd had: "... And then I got inside and there he was, wide open, and I could hear my daddy sayin' to me, "BANG HIM, SON...."

Once ditsy Flossie described how she kept her checkbook. If a check was for $50, she wrote $60 on the stub. If it was for $30, she recorded $35. Then every year before Christmas she'd ask the bank for her balance and she'd say, "Praise Jesus! Isn't He wonderful? Look at all this money!"

Rick and Flossie were a bit much, but they were good for us all. We think because of them, our whole church loosened up just a tad.

In our second church there was Bob. No, actually, there was only Bob's wife; he wouldn't come. But Florence said, "Why don't you come over for dinner? Then at least you can meet him."

We went. Bob said, "I don't have any friends but Florence, and I don't want any. If you want me to go to church I'll go, but I'll sit in the back and don't let anybody talk to me."

It was a deal, and Bob started sitting in the back, Sunday after Sunday....

Eventually Bob surrendered his heart to the Lord, and then he began to respond to friendships.

Then he became an usher. Then head usher!

Bob and Florence started attending our couples' group, and after a while he was made social chairman, in charge of the parties!

Bob couldn't carry a tune, but pretty soon he wanted to sing in the choir. Before long he could sing accurately the melody an octave lower—rats—and then eventually he could stay right on the bass. By the time we left the church Bob was singing in a mixed quartet, carrying the bass all by himself.

In our third pastorate we began traveling a little in ministry, and in Australia were invited to stay in the "prophets' chamber" of Tony and Laurelle, a young lawyer and his wife. It was a quiet little guest house behind their own home, and close to the sea. In between speaking at meetings we'd curl up on the couch, really tired, and a knock at the door would bring Laurelle bearing a tray of tea and cookies. She also lent us a foot massager. She paid for an Anne-facial. Tony and Laurelle are the personification of Romans 12:13: "Share with God's people who are in need. Practice hospitality."

In Pasadena there was a rather elegant lady in our church who'd lived most of her adult life in a lovely mansion. First she'd been nanny to the children, then caregiver when the mother sickened and died of cancer, then secretary-companion to the widower.

Marjorie had the gifts of helps; she was happiest doing things for people, and she was spending her life at it. She loved to bake for her pastor or make an orchid corsage from the estate's greenhouse for her pastor's wife. When our little son Nels arrived she began sewing him clothes, and she kept him outfitted for years.

Then old Mr. Baker died. The grown children, all married and prosperous, sold the mansion and dismissed Marjorie. That was that. No retirement, no parting gift—they just turned her out.

Marjorie, in her sixties, found a tiny upstairs apartment and began cleaning houses and working for sick people as a caregiver.

That was more than a quarter of a century ago, and she's lived ever since by frugality and God's miracle. But we've never heard her complain, not once. She has a hearty laugh, and she laughs a lot!

She's an aide for some of the church's children's choirs. She keeps their robes in order and helps with their parties. She's always blowing up balloons and making favors and dolls. She still sews clothes for little kids she loves, and she and her poodle visit convalescent homes every week to bring cheer. Marjorie has baked us tons of cookies over the years, for Christmas and any other occasion when she can get them to us.

And she's still a buddy of Nels. Recently she made him a pizza for his thirty-fifth birthday and ate it with Nels, now a cop, and his wife Heather and three little boys.

Marjorie is such a miracle, such a treasure, such a friend—when we think of her we want to cry.

6
CALIFORNIA HOMES

Basically, in Southern California we have three kinds of homes.

We have homes built by the first settlers who came west and built front porches on their houses so they could sit outside and talk to their neighbors.

We have homes built by the second wave, who put up town homes and condos with no porches—maybe just a peep hole in the front door. ("Who are you? Do I want to talk to you or don't I?")

And now we have brand new homes and condos with front porches on them so they can sit outside and talk to their neighbors!

An entire development of them is going up right now a block from where we live. We see the first people who've moved in talking to each other on their porches.

Do more pleasant relationships make happier people? We see little signs planted in the flowers in front of some of these new homes—signs like,

> SANDY FEET WELCOME
> YOU'RE AT THE BEACH!

and

> WELCOME TO PAPA AND NANA'S HOUSE
> GRANDKIDS SPOILED WHILE YOU WAIT

7

CAN YOUR CHILDREN BE YOUR FRIENDS?
SHOULD THEY BE?

There's a lot of confusion over whether our kids are to be our friends or not.

The two of us vote no.

Parents need to be *parents*, administering both the love and the discipline that our Heavenly Parent gives to us, His children. Says our book *Children Are Wet Cement,*

Children are really relieved to be treated as children. They can't stand the responsibility of adulthood yet. Sometimes you may not choose to explain your reason for dealing with them in a certain way. Many times when children ask, "Why can't I do so-and-so?" the best answer is "Because I'm your mother [or father], and I say you can't." This puts all the pressure on the parent, who is bigger and stronger and ought to have to take it!*

You guide them with strong love for maybe twenty years or so— in their teens gradually slacking off as you see them begin to follow the Lord, and coming on strong again when they regress and act childish.

The two of us loved telling our kids, "We can hardly wait till you're grown up, when we don't have to tell you what to do any more but we can just relax and enjoy you!"

None of our four seriously rebelled, and they each married wonderful Christian young people, with whom they are still

*Anne Ortlund, *Children Are Wet Cement* (Grand Rapids, Mich.: Fleming H. Revell, 1981), 90.

happily married and raising godly kids. Oh, how we thank the Lord! We can't take the credit. We see all around us how bad parents can have good children and good parents can have bad children. We just humbly thank Him.

When our children became adults we used to say, "Our kids are our best friends!" And it's true that they're our very *good* friends, with whom we freely play and party and act silly, and pray and discuss deeply and constantly affirm our affection for one another. The love of our children, grandchildren, and great-grandchildren is unspeakably precious to us, and when we're together as a family we say, "It just doesn't get any better than this!"

Sherry, our firstborn, is the one who usually sees that we're invited over for special days, and in between most often calls and says, "Let's all go out to eat tonight" or "Come see this movie with us" or some other spontaneous surprise of joy. And she and Walt always want to talk theology. They're great readers, and their growing knowledge overflows to us.

Margie, our second, lives in living color. She works the hardest at honoring us on our birthdays with huge family parties, and buying us the most tremendous gifts, and if we're sick sending us the biggest flower arrangements, and on all greeting cards writing us the shmooziest, gooshiest expressions of her adoration. It's all Margie's love language. When we're together she and John love to talk about the charming sayings and doings of our six grandchildren.

Ray, Jr., number three, befriends us aggressively as well. When he was college age he wrote his dad from the Holy Land,

"Hi, dear Dad: Today we visited the hills of Gilboa where the Philistines killed Saul and Jonathan. We read the account of their deaths and David's mourning in 1 and 2 Samuel. What a touching, moving picture of friendship and loyalty among men! Let's have that kind of loyalty and spirit among us! I love you as a devoted and admiring son.... Bud."

And to this day, though he's the one who lives a continent away, his zealous affection has never abated.

He and Nels, the caboose (who lives sixty miles away), both stay close by phone. Of our four, Nels is the one who's flattered us by insisting on our being at the hospital when each of his three sons was born. A while back he took his dad camping overnight; he brought all the food and gear and did the cooking. This coming Saturday Nels, our police officer, is taking his dad with him for the day in his patrol car.

And our four in-laws, Walt, John, Jani, and Heather, are not only constant in their expressions of love to us but have taught all their children to do the same. Our cup runs over!

Then shouldn't we say that all these offspring of ours are our best friends? We don't think so. In each case there's one ingredient that's missing.

Proverbs says many times that best friends take the privilege of rebuking one another:

Better is open rebuke than hidden love.
Wounds from a friend can be trusted, but an enemy
    multiplies kisses.

PROVERBS 27:5, 6

Through trial and error—*major* error on our part!—we've

learned that rebuking our grown children is off-limits. They would be the first to agree that the time for their parents' rebuking them was over when they became adults. (And there is *no* right time to rebuke a grandchild, unless you're temporarily or permanently taking over the function of parent.)

Sometimes the two of us have thought, My goodness, we have all this amazing wisdom crammed inside us, and we could spare them from getting into so much trouble....

No.

Prayer is our constant recourse, but we ourselves get into trouble unless we shut our mouths.

And, actually, it's certainly more fun to be spared the responsibility of rebuking, and just relax and enjoy them and watch the Holy Spirit do it!

So we've figured out that we can be 99 percent best friends, and then make this our philosophy:

Each generation should be trained through childhood by earthly parents or guardians, and after that their Heavenly Parent takes over.

And His parenting is far better, with guaranteed results:

He who began a good work in you will carry it on to completion until the day of Christ Jesus.

PHILIPPIANS 1:6

There are three levels of friendships:

Best friends

Guest friends

Pest friends

8
CAN GOOD FRIENDSHIPS DIE?

Friendship is different from kinship. If you're related to someone by blood, not by marriage, you automatically have a kinship relationship, just by being born.

But friendship? It has far greater potential.

There is a friend who sticks closer than a brother.

PROVERBS 18:24

There's nothing automatic about a friendship. It calls for proactive commitment. It takes a lot of work and a lot of time, and without constant maintenance it can easily be lost.

We can think of a couple we used to be friends with, but negligence has caused the bond to erode. In the last several years we've run into each other twice, and all four of us were genuinely delighted. We even said, "Let's get together!" and we meant it. But then we didn't.

The fact is, the longer you live, the more people you meet! You can't keep every past friendship going for life or you could never nurture new ones. It's important that some friendships deepen and become lifelong, but it's also inevitable that others slough off and are lost.

So be it. God will guide the path of every friendship, and dead ones should bring fond memories without guilt.

Can good friendships die? They can.

But don't let them go hastily or in anger; friendships are too hard to come by, too precious.

A really good new one takes a very long time to develop.

9
MEN AND FRIENDSHIPS
[Written by Ray]

God in His kindness has let the two of us minister to people all over the world, and we sense people are pretty much alike: they have the same joys, fears, hopes, and problems.

But it's interesting over the world to observe men and their friendships, and I see a difference between those in other countries and in America.

I was in Malawi, speaking at a conference for national pastors. During the week a fellow speaker and I really clicked; one black African, one white American, we laughed and prayed and served together.

One day we were strolling along enjoying our new friendship, and he reached over and took my hand. I tell you, I was shocked! Hot flashes came over me as I looked around to see if anybody was watching.

We Westerners aren't used to showing affection that way, are we! In our macho society guys keep a safe distance from other guys; consequently many of us are lonely. We haven't developed the art of expressing friendship.

When Anne and I have a conference for a church in a small town in America I like to ask the pastor, about mid-morning, to take me to the local coffee shop. Sure enough, pretty soon the men start coming in from the shops or fields for a coffee break. They throw their quarters into a receptacle, pour their own coffee, and sit down at a long table. They've done it for years.

And do they gather to share their hurts, their insecurities, their joys, their dreams? Not on your life. They crab about the lousy government, or they critique a game on TV the night before—the stupid coaches and the ump's stupid calls. They get through all their grumbling and then it's time to go back to work again. And their morning ritual has proved they're real guys.

The comic strip character Charlie Brown was asked what he was going to be when he grew up. He thought about the men he knew and he answered, "Lonely."

Most American men, I think, are even lonely at home. They seldom air anything deeply personal, not even to their wives. A psychologist asked a couple I know who'd been married twenty years to sit down once a day and talk to each other with no one else around. No radio, no television—for twenty minutes a day, seven days in a row, just talk. The husband told me it was a disaster; it was threatening and embarrassing and he couldn't handle it.

Why is there this male fear of openness and resistance to bonding?

First, men have been taught by our Western culture that a "real man" conceals his true self.

I read about two golfers who'd been playing together every week for years. Then one had to have major surgery. A couple of months later he was well enough and they met again on the first tee.

"Heard you been sick," said one.

The other said, "Yeah, but let's tee off. I'm gonna beat the pants off you."

One didn't know how to care, and the other didn't know how to share.

I remember hearing that "cowboys don't cry." That's silly; have you listened to a cowboy song? "The missus has left me, *my dogie's dead...." They're crying all over the place.*

But "real men" have this image of plunging into the dangers of life tight-lipped and steely-eyed. What a shame.

The Bible shows how David, a masterful king and brilliant commander of troops, was also tender and open. Read his psalms, and see how David lays bare his soul in front of all of us.

And, of course, look at Jesus, the perfect God-man. He's both tough and tender. He could courageously face money changers and whip them out of the temple; and yet He is "touched with the feeling of our infirmities" (Hebrews 4:15, KJV).

Second, our Western culture tells us that "real men" must always look like winners. In sports or business or whatever, real guys never lose. Packer coach Vince Lombardi's favorite line was "Winning isn't everything—it's the only thing." Or the sign on the college gym locker room reads, "Nice guys finish last."

So "real men" must appear to win—and if they lose, they stuff it. And yet we all lose! A great ball hitter may hit .350 during a season, but that means he missed the ball two-thirds of the time. The idea that "real men" always win is not only wrong, it's wicked.

The Bible tells us to "get real"—"All have sinned and fall short of the glory of God" (Romans 3:23).

This verse says we've all missed the mark; we shot at the target, but we all fell short—every one of us. Now we need comfort and encouragement. And the Lord Himself promises us, "My grace is sufficient for you, for my power is made perfect in weakness" (2 Corinthians 12:9).

You 'fess up, and God takes up. All of God's great men have been ordinary men—even losers—who counted on an extraordinary Savior and God.

Third, there's the idea in Western culture that "real men" don't admit needs or ask for help.

Did you ever hunt for an unknown address, and the map is confusing and you wander around for fifteen minutes? And your wife says, "Dear, let's go ask that gas station." Will you do it? Never!

When Anne and I walk into a store she goes straight to a clerk and asks for a certain item. Me? I have to find it on my own.

So we men sit in a church board meeting with aching hearts, and we go out afterward as aching as when we came in. And all the while there were godly men sitting all around us—and available. We come in needy and we go out needy and we call it fellowship! We may even read Scripture together—something like, "Carry each other's burdens, and in this way you will fulfill the law of Christ" (Galatians 6:2).

Fourth, we males have this fear of openness and a resistance to bonding because we're sinners. We're like our first parents, Adam and Eve, who tried to hide behind some trees from God, and then put on those ridiculous fig leaves to hide from each other. As soon as they sinned their relationships got screwed up. And we descendants, every one, suffer from self-imposed loneliness. Our faces seem to say, "Private; no admittance." And it's no fun.

How does this affect us men? Most of us tend to be bland, colorless, and inhibited. Once in a while we meet a fellow who's free and joyous and open, and we think, "If only I dared to be like that...."

And our inhibitions are stressful, and we live shorter lives then the women, who are more open than we are. I'm told that *for every one hundred women over the age of sixty-five or seventy, there are only about seventy-five men.*

Let me ask you: Who knows you through and through? Do you have a friend with whom you can share your plans, your temptations, your dreams, your failures, your fears, your joys? If you have one you're doing well. If you say you have two, you're doing great. If you say you have three, you're lying. Or so they say.

How can we men cross the fear barrier and find true friends?

First, as we've written elsewhere in this book, start by being a friend of Christ. He said to His disciples, "I have called you friends." He could say this because He is the friend of sinners. If you give your life to Christ you're counted as "in Christ," and you're absolutely accepted.

So now, be His friend. Do what He asks of you. Live each day with your friend. Talk to Him. Walk with Him. In your special times of need rush to Him for help. Be Christ's friend, and take advantage of Him!

Second, be a friend with your wife. Take time to share with her your feelings, and listen carefully as she expresses her feelings. Make a deal with her that you want her to be your best friend, and that from now on you're going to let her in on all your life, and you want the same from her. It may truly be a "fresh start" in your marriage!

Anne and I were traveling down a local street once and I was feeling needy. I said, "Anne, I need to tell you how I'm feeling. I sense I'm such a failure! I feel so weak."

As I was pouring out my insecurities to her she interrupted,

"Ray, that's not true. You're being foolish. The Bible says—"

I said, "Hey, Anne, I know that; I just needed to share with you what's going on in my heart. Just listen to me." She said, "Oh, I'm sorry." And she heard me out.

Several weeks later we were on the same stretch of road, and Anne opened herself up to me in the very same way. And I interrupted her saying, "Anne, you know that's not true. Now snap out of it. Listen to what the Word of God says," and I nailed her with Scripture. Dear Anne said, "Ray, all I want you to do is listen to me." Of course I got the message, apologized and listened!

Here's an Arabian proverb:

A friend is one to whom one may pour out all the contents of one's heart, chaff and grain together, knowing that the gentlest of hands will take and sift it, keep what is worth keeping, and with the breath of kindness blow the rest away.

First Peter 3:7 says,

Husbands, ... be considerate as you live with your wives, and treat them with respect as the weaker partner and as heirs with you of the gracious gift of life, so that nothing will hinder your prayers.

Study this wife of yours. She's far more wonderful than you realize. Listen to her. Best friends do that.

Last, have a special buddy, and also be in a small group of five or six men to read the Word, pray, and share your lives together.

It takes time to have a friend. It takes time for a small group

of guys to hang in there and become true friends in Christ.
Sharing around God's Word makes it stable and rich.

For about thirty years I've discipled at least one small group
of guys each year, with each one committed to start his own
small group when we're through. Anne has done the same with
women. I cannot tell you how these people have helped us,
taught us, encouraged us, prayed for us, and loved us—and we,
them.

[Anne's postscript] Let me tell you about Ray's two friends,
Lenox and Ed.

Years ago when he was pastoring in Pasadena, Ray regularly
attended a prayer meeting of other local pastors, and he and
Lenox, one of the others, were especially attracted to one another.
They began meeting for lunches and their hearts became knit.

Lenox was a middle-aged, huge, ex-Princeton football player,
gentle as a lamb, deep, and loving. The more meaningful their
friendship became, the tougher it was to realize some day other
ministries would tear them apart. Sure enough, eventually Lenox
took a pastorate in the Midwest, but their friendship has continued strongly by phone and e-mails, by exchanges of books,
ideas, and prayer needs, and by long travels occasionally to see
each other.

Just the same, when Lenox moved away Ray felt the need for
a new eyeball-to-eyeball friend. This time he prayed about sug-
gesting such a thing to Ed, a completely different type—a quiet,
sharp businessman turned missions leader he'd known well for
twenty years. He took him to lunch.

"Ed," he said, "would you be my buddy? Could we meet regularly together? I'm looking for someone who can walk around

in my life anywhere, and ask any questions, and pray for me and hold me accountable, and I'll do the same with him. What do you think?"

For twelve years so far Ed and Ray have met monthly for lunch, sharing their hearts as peers—brothers in Christ—in absolute commitment. They've prayed each other through many dark valleys; they've reprimanded and applauded each other; they've wept and laughed, shared theological books and ideas, and sought advice and comfort from each other.

Ray is a man with many friends, but I know he's wiser and happier because of the loves of Lenox and Ed.

10
ONE ORDINARY MORNING
[Written by Ray]

One ordinary morning I was reading my Bible and I came to Psalm 133:1:

How good and pleasant it is when brothers live together in unity!

And I thought how there is true goodness and pleasantness in a friendship that's around the Lord.

The phone rang, and a voice said, "Hey, Ray, how are you? This is Neill Robbins. I was just thinking about you. Have you got a minute?"

I said, "Neill! Dear guy, sure, I've got lots of minutes for you."

Neill and I have been friends for over forty years; my heart has always met with his. He's a loving, caring man, and this morning his Southern drawl made memories of our times together come flooding back into my soul. We had a great time catching up and encouraging one another. Then he wanted to talk about a man he'd been counseling and wanted my take on how to help him.

That half hour on the phone was so "good and pleasant." Then I went back to Psalm 133 and read on:

*[Unity between brothers] is like precious oil poured on the
head,*
running down on the beard,
running down on Aaron's beard,
down upon the collar of his robes.
It is as if the dew of Hermon
were falling on Mount Zion.
For there the Lord bestows his blessing,
Even life forevermore.

*I said, "O Lord, I feel soaked in oil, drenched in dew." Dear
Neill!*

The heading of Psalm 133 tells us that the writer was David.
He'd been anointed king three times (1 Samuel 16:13; 2 Samuel
2:4; 5:3)! He knew about being anointed, and he compared
unity among the brothers to the sweet-scented oil poured out
extravagantly over the head of Aaron the high priest. In either
case, anointing a priest or a king was an event of high joy and
loud celebration. It was party time! And the fragrance of the
lavishly applied oil smelled to high heaven—God enjoys unity
more than anybody!

David's second likeness to unity was quiet, but in its way just
as delicious. He'd lived plenty of years in desert heat and spent
many a hot, hot day with sheep. So he also knew how "good and
pleasant" it was when the evening dews came down. They
dampened his clothes, his face, his hair; what coolness, what
relief!

So in our harsh world, hot with tensions, a godly friendship
is like dew that moistens and soaks the dry heart.

My friend Neill called! I couldn't get over it.

I was alone; Anne was out on a retreat with the gals she'd been discipling.

And then, can you believe it— the phone rang: "Hey, Ray, this is Neill Robbins.... Got a minute?"

It was oil on my head, and for half an hour it ran down me and I dripped. And it was like dew that cooled and refreshed.

Ah, true unity in friendship is "good and pleasant"!

11
WHO *NOT* TO BE FRIENDS WITH

Let's get this subject over with before we go any further, and then get on with all the positive.

The relationships in your life affect you so strongly, they actually shape you and mold you. "Lie down with dogs and you'll get up with fleas."

That's why the Word of God is so full of warnings about what people to stay away from:

> Blessed is the man who does not
> walk in the counsel of the wicked
> or stand in the way of sinners
> or sit in the seat of mockers.
>
> PSALM 1:1

A very talented twelve-year-old keyboardist we knew started hanging out with gay teenagers. He recently died horribly of AIDS.

"Friendship evangelism" is effective only if the operative word is "evangelism," not "friendship." It's the job of each of us who are Christ's undershepherds to go, as He assigns us, and penetrate the horrors of the Wild Lands to snatch back a lost sheep—but then get it out of there fast.

> And when he finds it he joyfully puts it on his shoulder [he bears happily the burdens of this newly rescued one] and goes home.
>
> LUKE 15:5

Home is where they both normally belong; it's the only safe place.

The power of gangs has destroyed great numbers of kids.

The seduction of peer pressure has destroyed great numbers of adults.

We throw around the words "love" and "forgive" in absolute naivete, ignorant of the ruthless power not only of sin but of sinners. Warns 1 Corinthians 15:33, "Do not be misled. Bad company corrupts good character. Come back to your senses!"

Cute teenagers—likeable, fun adults—these are among Satan's most effective tools in this world to lure others to himself and to misery.

In Old Testament Proverbs, our heavenly Father's "wisdom book," He writes strong advice like this to each of His children—us:

My son, if sinners entice you,
    do not give in to them.
If they say, "Come along with us...,"
My son, do not go along with them,
    do not set foot on their paths.

PROVERBS 1:10-15

The New Testament is just as clear:

What fellowship can light have with darkness?...
What does a brother have in common with an unbeliever?...
Therefore come out from them and be separate,
    says the Lord.
Touch no unclean thing

2 CORINTHIANS 6:14-17

Satan has persuaded Christians to scorn these warnings, picturing the "separate" ones as holier-than-thou goody-goodies piously drawing their skirts around themselves. The devil whispers in Christians' ears that Jesus was the friend of sinners, and their muddied thinking forgets that the holy Son of God was unique—the only One strong enough to be "tempted ... just as we are, yet without sin" (Hebrews 5:15).

We tend to think we can handle it.

So we wallow around continually with unbelievers—not witnessing, just wallowing. And we pick up their thinking and their culture; we intermarry with them; we become indistinguishable from them. Satan has conquered us. We're now intimidated and impotent.

Feel the white heat of James, describing Christians who two-time the Lord:

> You adulterous people, don't you know that friendship with the world is hatred toward God?
>
> JAMES 4:4

Dear believer who's picked up this book, any writing on friendship needs to include this part of the truth.

Yes, it's only a part. God writes to us through Paul,

> The Lord's servant ... must be kind to everyone.... Those who oppose him [notice the stance of a non-Christian we can expect] he must gently instruct, in the hope that God will grant them repentance leading them to a knowledge of the truth, and that they will come to their senses and escape the trap of the devil, who has taken them captive to do his will.
>
> 2 TIMOTHY 2:24-26, brackets ours

Should we be kind? Yes. Appealing? If possible. Looking for opportunities? Always. But fraternizing and cozy? No.

"Do not love the world or anything in the world.... For everything in the world [is summed up in] the cravings of sinful man, the lust of his eyes and the boasting of what he has and does" (1 John 2:15, 16).

The two of us shudder when we read this description of what's in the world. Oh, the enticements can be strong, can't they!

"The woman saw that the fruit of the tree was good for food and pleasing to the eye and also desirable for gaining wisdom" (Genesis 3:6).

Spirit of God, give us two writers and this reader a holy fear of the world and the flesh and the devil.

Nevertheless—and this is a huge nevertheless—

God has a yearning, brooding, aching, longing in His heart for the world of sinners to be saved. Through His dear Son's blood shed on the cross,

> God was reconciling the world to himself.... And he has committed to us the message of reconciliation. We are therefore Christ's ambassadors, as though God were making his appeal through us. We implore you on Christ's behalf: Be reconciled to God.
>
> 2 CORINTHIANS 5:19, 20

We had lovely neighbors next door to us for fifteen years, who grew to love us but not Him. For all of those fifteen years we prayed for them by name every single night. We had many meals with them. We gave them our books. We gave them our updated itineraries so they'd know where we were when we were traveling.

We chatted across the lawns. We told them when we were on the radio. We got our small groups for years to pray for them, too. From vacations we wrote postcards.

On a recent birthday card to Al we took extra pages to spell out the gospel again. Did he finally take it into his heart? Several days later he dropped dead on the eighteenth hole.

We spent more time with dear, grieving, failing Gloria. We pled! "I can't change religions," she said—though, basically, she had none. When we were gone, did she change her mind? Shortly afterward she stopped breathing.

Paul to the Ephesians: "Pray also for me, that whenever I open my mouth ... I may declare [the gospel] fearlessly, as I should" (Ephesians 6:19, 20). Paul to the Colossians: "Be wise in the way you act toward outsiders; make the most of every opportunity" (Colossians 4:5, 6).

Do you see the difference? God's Word says you're to relate to outsiders as outsiders: "For what do righteousness and wickedness have in common? Or what fellowship can light have with darkness?" (2 Corinthians 6:14).

None at all!

And yet with great tenderness and entreating we're to reach out to the darkness, remembering that that's where we used to be—"but we were washed" (1 Corinthians 6:11).

Then,

Become blameless and pure, children of God without fault in a crooked and depraved generation, in which you shine like stars in the universe as you hold out the Word of life.

PHILIPPIANS 2:15, 16

Distinct from the world but never angry at them, blaming them, belittling them. They're like the paralytic in Mark 2; they have no Holy Spirit, so they're helpless, they can't be righteous—they just need to be tenderly carried to Jesus.

[Anne writing] Ray remarked to me a while back, "I don't know enough guys who drink and cuss and sleep around." And it was bothering him.

Then somebody gave him a membership to a local health club. It was just the ticket! He prays while he works out and asks the Lord to open doors to the hearts of those guys.

It's a big club and Ray doesn't know them all—but somehow the word gets around that he's "the Rev."

Recently he went up to run on the rooftop track. There was only one fellow already there, running a long way ahead. But eventually he stopped, and when Ray caught up to him he asked, "What do you do when your life is falling apart?"! And for half an hour God didn't let anyone else come up to the track, and the two of them stood there and talked, Ray with his arm around him and sometimes praying.

That's why he's a member of the health club.

But there needs to be a postscript here. The New Testament names three other kinds of people to avoid, and they're actually right inside the church.

Please, don't cut any of them off hastily! Continually clothe yourself in gentleness and patience, bearing with one another (Colossians 3:12, 13). Furthermore, seek to restore them without sliding down into the same pit (Galatians 6:1-5).

But if these groups stubbornly continue in their ways, then avoid them:

Group one: Christians who are deliberately malicious: "I urge you, brothers [writes Paul], to watch out for those who cause divisions and put obstacles in your way that are contrary to the teaching you have learned. Keep away from them" (Romans 16:17).

Group two: Christians who are deliberately worldly: "There will be terrible times in the last days. People will be lovers of themselves, lovers of money, boastful, proud,... having a form of godliness but denying its power. Have nothing to do with them" (2 Timothy 3:1-5).

Group three: Christians who are lazy and rebellious: "We command you, brothers, to keep away from every brother who is idle and does not live according to the teaching you received from us" (2 Thessalonians 3:6).

Still, pray that the breaking of fellowship may be temporary and remedial: "Yet do not regard him as an enemy, but warn him as a brother" (1 Thessalonians 3:15).

Your heart still loves such as these, and you pray for the day when they've repented and changed their behavior and you're friends again.

Conclusion, then: All your relationships, whether with unbelievers or with believers, must be under the guidance of Jesus Christ. You'll get into big trouble if you don't bring every one of them under His lordship and control.

He will always lead you perfectly to stay away from this person (Acts 8:21-23) and to come close to that one (Acts 8:29-35).

The King James Version of Ephesians 5:15 tells you to "walk circumspectly." "Circumspectly" means looking around, every step you take. Like a cat after a rain, crossing a street full of puddles. He lifts each paw; he looks before he puts it down.

In all your friendships, in all your relationships, God wants your paws clean.

Pray about all this a lot.

12
P.S. MORE ORTLUND FRIENDS

The two of us have friends who are geographically distant but close in our hearts:

Don and Elaine in northern California, who stuck by us years ago when we were in trouble; Kim and Julie, young housewives in Bozeman, Montana, touched at one of our conferences; Kathy and Faye in Paducah, Kentucky, whose lives spark ours from time to time; Gary and Jackie in Clearwater Beach, Florida, with whom we instantly connect whenever our paths cross....

Larry and Penny in Goshen, Indiana, who helped us on a missionary trip, have had an open house so their friends could learn about our work, have been team members for several of our conferences, and have faithfully encouraged us and shared their lives with ours....

Then we have mementos around our home which weren't chosen by any decorator—they've been gifts from Drew, Becky, Mary Alice, Margie, Dad long ago, friends in Iran, missionaries in Africa, Mother long ago, the Board of LIFE Ministries, the Board of Haven Ministries, Sherry and Walt, Margie and John, Ray, Jr., and Jani, Nels and Heather, our four children together, a friend in India, friends in Afghanistan, missionaries in Brazil, a friend in England, a pastor in Australia, an old lady Ray used to call on, a Filipina in whose Manila home we taught the Bible, Betty, Beulah, Melinda, Peggy, M.J., church women in northern Canada, Eskimos in Barrow, Alaska, several of our small groups, John and Trude, Chuck and Sharon Kay, Ken and Jan, Bill and Ruth, Peter and Gail....

Some of the gifts are humble, some are wonderful, but we cherish each of them: They were given by friends.

Part II

How To
Strengthen Your
Relational Muscles

Portrait of a Friend II*

A friend is patient. He under-speaks, he over-listens.

A friend is kind. He under-assumes, he over-clarifies.

A friend doesn't envy. He's content with what he is and has, and wishes others the same.

A friend doesn't boast. He knows that God alone is on the throne.

A friend isn't proud. He approaches people not with "Here I am" but "There you are!"

A friend isn't rude. He sees others not as things to be used but as people.

A friend isn't self-seeking. He demands fairness and equality for others but never for himself.

A friend isn't easily angered. He asks the Lord to wash away malice, use anger to reform, and then bring forgiveness and peace.

*From 1 Corinthians 13:4-8

A friend keeps no record of wrongs. He just repays the wrongdoer with deeds of kindness.

A friend doesn't delight in evil but rejoices with the truth. He seeks openness, to know and to be known.

A friend always protects. His love covers all his friend's misdeeds.

A friend always trusts. He is responsible for, accountable to.

A friend always hopes. Through down times he's optimistic.

A friend always perseveres. He under-promises, he over-delivers.

A friend never fails. He's Christlike!

13
BE PATIENT

The soul of Jonathan was knit with the soul of David,
and Jonathan loved him as his own soul.

1 SAMUEL 18:1, KJV

Aren't there many people you'd like to have your heart knit
to? You think of those with whom you'd be thrilled to have a
David-Jonathan friendship.

But knitting takes time. It takes time for a bone to knit. It
takes time for a sweater to be knit. It takes time for a friendship to be knit.

May this fact give you pause, but not stop you. It probably
means you can't have dozens of good friends, but give
enough time in your life for at least two or three.

Everyone needs several really close friends. God made you
for that. Paul prayed that believers might be "comforted,
being knit together in love" (Colossians 2:2, KJV).

Investing enough time for lives to knit together means
developing patience. In the Scriptures "patience" is often
translated "longsuffering," which gives you a better idea. To
become a good friend means to learn to put up with a lot—
cheerfully, because it's worth it.

For instance, take the two of us writing this book! And
especially as we labored over this chapter on patience—it took
heaps of patience on the part of both of us!

"How about using the illustration of our friend Sophie's
patience with her husband Arch?" Anne throws in. "He was
a drinking, cheating, no-good bum, and she was patient for

thirty years until he got saved and became a really good man."

"That's too extreme," Ray answers. "I can't buy that ... What if we deal with the aspect of the trust it takes to wait for a friend to open up and get real before the friendship can get deep and good? We can use our T.S. Eliot quote."

"That would overlap with our chapter on 'Always Trust,'" says Anne.

We go back and forth on ideas for a long time, definitely starting to lose our patience with each other—!—and then it occurs to us that we could use ourselves as the illustration in this chapter of two friends needing patience! What softened our hearts was remembering Colossians 3:13, and seeking to apply it to our own attitudes in this situation: "Bear with each other and forgive whatever grievances you may have against one another. Forgive as the Lord forgave you."

To have a deep, rich friendship takes patience. We all need to take the time to hear each other out, to consider each other's viewpoints, to pray, to wait, to soften.

Remember—the finished product of knitting is beautiful.

14
BE KIND

Absorb the costs of a friendship.

Yes, including the financial costs.

A friendship can be coming along so beautifully—and with such satisfaction to each—and suddenly some money situation rears its ugly head. Money has caused many a friendship to go south.

Whenever finances come between you and your friend, *you* pay—and save the friendship. But it wasn't your fault? Pay anyway, and pay gladly. All money belongs to the Lord, and He is watching. If that payment is a burden to you, you may be sure God will reimburse you.

And then forget it. "Love ... keeps no records of wrongs" (1 Corinthians 13:5).

The only lay person Paul wrote a letter to which got included in Holy Scriptures was his "dear friend and fellow worker," Philemon (verse 1).

Philemon was a wealthy man; the Colossian church met in his large home. But he had a bad slave, who stole from him and ran away. The slave ran all the way to Rome, where somehow Paul, in prison there for the gospel, led him to accept the Lord. The little book of Philemon is Paul's letter to accompany the slave as Paul sent him back, now converted, to his master.

But Philemon's blood pressure could have risen. Should he take this fellow back just because now he's a Christian? The guy still owes him all that money.

Paul jumps in ahead of Philemon's reaction: "Whatever he owes you," writes Paul, "send me the bill. I'm happy to pay it back myself."

Well, is rich Philemon going to ask money from his dear friend Paul who's in prison? Of course not—but Paul had defused the bomb. Nevertheless, Paul wasn't playing games; his offer was sincere.

[Ray writing] *In Pasadena I was leading a discipleship group of five guys who were all seminary students preparing for ministry. Those fellows really loved each other.*

One day one of them was so discouraged, he said he was quitting seminary. He had a wife and a baby and didn't see how he could afford to keep going.

"You can't quit!" the others all said with one voice. "Keep going! We'll give you all the money you need! Ask us any time, but don't quit!"

Now, the other four were just as broke as the first, but in that moment the Holy Spirit endowed them with a greater measure of the gift of faith.

My friend kept going from semester to semester, he never had to ask the guys for money, he graduated, and today he's an outstanding pastor, known all over the country.

We know two couples who dearly love each other. One is a wealthy young businessman; the other is a young pastor just scraping by. The pastor needed a hefty sum of money for a ministry project; his buddy the businessman supplied it— but he thought it was a loan to be repaid when the project perhaps generated income; the pastor thought it was a gift.

Eventually they figured out the shocking misunderstanding. What happened?

The issue was dropped. They are still the best of friends.

Praise the Lord.

15
DON'T ENVY

Don't expect fairness from other people.

Forget "tit for tat."

We were supposed to have lunch with someone recently and went to the wrong restaurant and we missed each other; it was totally our fault. She was someone we didn't know and wouldn't have offended for the world. But the relationship ground to a halt when she phoned and demanded that we come right down that day to her area (about forty minutes from us, one way) rather than finding another time to meet again halfway.

"You didn't show," she said. "I was at the correct place. Now the least you can do is drive down today to my city to meet me; this is the day I saved time for you."

She was absolutely right in her facts but wrong in her spirit.

Fight valiantly for fairness for others—that's another subject— but never demand it for yourself. Demanding equality loses a lot of potential friends.

"Do not say, 'I'll do to him as he has done to me; I'll pay that man back for what he did'" (Proverbs 24:29).

"Our fever for equality," writes Gustave Thibou, "is one of the deepest and most serious ills of our age.... In the end, nobody finds himself able to stand being unequal to anyone else in anything."*

This insistent groping for equality means that sick people envy the healthy; poor people envy the rich; old people envy the young; homely people envy the good-looking; and

*Paul Tournier: *Escape from Loneliness,* 118.

everybody resents how he is because he thinks that in some area "fate" didn't make him on a par with somebody else.

Don't you see that this "insistent groping for equality" puts the spotlight right on our view of God? Either you trust God and believe that He knows what He's doing and you accept what He metes out to you, or you "get mad at God."

Our view of God means everything in how we treat other people.

To make enemies, let unfairness and inequalities in your life really bug you.

To make enemies, always demand your own rights.

Fear others' taking advantage of you.

Fear their outsmarting you.

Fear their outstripping you.

Send scathing letters to demand equal opportunities for yourself.

Protest everything; correct everyone.

In God's temporarily unequal and unfair world, exhaust yourself demanding equality and fairness.

To make friends, relax and trust God's care for you. (Everything begins with you and God.)

To make friends, let yourself be wronged (1 Corinthians 6:7); never take revenge, let God do it (Romans 12:19, 20).

To make friends, give generously to others, knowing God will supply back to you (Proverbs 11:24, 25).

To make friends, freely accept one another, just as Christ accepts you (Romans 15:7).

To make friends, don't envy; be content with your own lot (Philippians 4:11).

We learned a lesson in contentment the other day. We went to have lunch with our dear friends Wen and Ginny, with whom we have a long history of closeness.

Wen sat there looking tanned and handsome and ready for nine holes. But he's actually very near the end of his life, and his doctor has finally taken him off all medication except for pain.

"It's all right," said Wen, looking at us calmly, steadily, and wrinkling up his eyes in a little smile. "God has given me a wonderfully full and happy life. And He's in charge."

To make friends, fix your eyes on Jesus so you can forget ego. Think of Mother Teresa, and exhaust yourself in loving others, in overcoming evil with good.

Bleed for your friends, and never notice the blood.

16
DON'T BOAST

A person who knows that only God is on the throne has a great start in being a friend. He understands that without Christ he has nothing, although in Christ he has everything. He can reach out to his Christian brother in humility and gratitude, knowing that what Christ has given him He's also given his brother—both are just recipients of His wonderful grace in all its fullness—and neither is above the other.

Oh, this is fabulous news! What Christ gives each one of us is all we have, and it's all we need. "It is because of [God] that you are in Christ Jesus.... Let him who boasts boast in the Lord" (1 Corinthians 1:30, 31).

Our friend Ed Fischer knows that the Lord is on the throne.

When we came to pastor Lake Avenue Congregational Church in Pasadena, Ed was the choir director and his dear Leta was one of the sopranos.

But Ed wasn't just into music, he was into the Lord. His heart was always fervent, and his choir was a cheering section for God.

What sweet fellowship we had together!—in prayer, in fun times (they'd have us over for dinner and Leta would beat the pants off us in Ping-Pong), and in all the church activities: if the door was open they were there.

When we ministered overseas they were at the airport to see us off and then to welcome us home. Our hearts were bound up in friendship because God was first in their lives, and God was first in ours.

Never, never have we heard Ed Fischer boast.

We remember a time at the close of a church service when the Holy Spirit was resting heavily upon us all—and Ed did what the rest of us had only wanted to do: Without any invitation he came out of the choir loft and knelt in front. He did it simply because his heart was tender and obedient to God.

The time came when we needed a full-time minister of music and Ed had a teaching position at a local college.... We hired a man, and Ed joined the bass section. He was just as comfortable following as leading, because he just wasn't a boastful person.

And for half a century, now, Ed has either led the sanctuary choir or sung in it, and his voice is still firm and true and his faithfulness unabating. Leta died not long ago of Alzheimer's disease, but Ed has been faithful in attendance before, during, and since.

"... Of whom the world is not worthy...."

Larry Crabb writes, "We promote another's holiness by pursuing our own. Our private choices affect the kind of influence we have on people."*

All your friendships flow out of your friendship with God. From Him come the deeps that make you valuable to others. Then you see how crucial it is to keep a vital, cleansed, moment-by-moment relationship with Him.

Your friendship with God defines you, and it determines everything about your life: who you are, what you do, what company you keep. Guard carefully your holy disciplines of prayer, Scripture reading, and worship.

---

*Larry Crabb, *The Safest Place on Earth* (Nashville: Tenn. Word, 1999), 128.

You who have no mother to love you,
    and yet crave for love,
        God will be as a mother.

You who have no brother to help you,
    and have so much need of support,
        God will be your brother.

You who have no friends to comfort you,
    and stand so much in need of consolation,
        God will be your friend.*

Have a passion for Him only! Let all the emptiness of your ego and self-boasting be swallowed up in the fullness of God Himself. "May I never boast except in the cross of the Lord Jesus Christ" (Galatians 6:14).

*from *Gold Dust,* a little centuries-old book of unknown origin.

17
DON'T BE PROUD

Don't try to always be right.

Our dear Christian psychologist friend tells this story on himself.

Early in his practice a woman came to him absolutely distraught. "I can't live with my husband one day longer," she said.

"What's the problem?" asked our friend.

"He doesn't need me," she said. "He is sufficient unto himself. He's the source of all wisdom and knowledge. I can't tell him anything; he's insufferable! When he speaks he acts as if the wisdom of the universe has just opened its mouth. I've had it!"

Our friend asked, "What does your husband do?"

"He's a Christian psychologist," she said....

Our friend says, suddenly he saw himself! He felt as if the prophet Nathan had just proclaimed, "Thou art the man."

When the woman left he went out and walked the streets of the city for hours—for most of the night. And God began to reveal to him what kind of man he was, what kind of a friend he was, what kind of a husband he'd been to his wife—and what he needed to become.

He was softened, broken. He humbled himself, and then God could make him great.

Humility, softness, makes friends.

People who are "always right" are often friendless. They're frustrating; they're intimidating; they're humiliating; and they build walls between themselves and others.

Of course it's good to be right! It's wonderful to see clearly and come to correct judgments. But how often and how quickly being right can lead to being self-righteous and mean!

Catch from the Proverbs what may be the better choice of what we're to do with all that elevating information:

"A man of knowledge uses words with restraint" (17:27).

"A prudent man keeps his knowledge to himself" (12:23).

"The heart of the righteous weighs his answers" (15:28).

[Anne writing] I saw myself recently in one of Dr. Paul Tournier's sentences, as he described a wife: "She was a strong person, logical, one who broke [her husband's] spirit because she was in the right and because she held his errors against him."*

Ray and I are both verbal, and as I told you before I love to debate, and for years I did. And at the end of some of our debates there I'd be, so *right*—and so lonely! I'd won the battle (or so I thought) but lost the war.

I laughed as I read this quote from Dave Barry: "I argue very well. Ask any of my remaining friends. I can win an argument on any topic. People know this and steer clear of me at parties. Often, as a sign of their great respect, they don't even invite me."*

Ray is far more relational than I, and it took years of his influence before I began to weigh those corrections and pronouncements always on the tip of my tongue and to ask

*Paul Tournier, *Escape from Loneliness,* p. 142.
*Miami Herald.

myself, "What effect will this have on the listener? How will it make him feel? How can my words build a bridge between us? How can I lift him up?"

Being right is especially dangerous when the issue is doctrinal: Maybe we have a beef with someone in our church, because he just doesn't see what we see. Of course we don't want to budge an inch, and we quickly get critical and proud—even unconsciously putting ourselves up and the other down.

In this case Romans 14 is really a friend-making chapter! "The man [who holds a certain view] must not look down on him who does not, and the man who does not ... must not condemn the man who does, for God has accepted him" (v. 3).

This chapter isn't speaking of basic doctrine determining whether a person is saved or not; Romans 14 is talking about weaknesses within Christ's body. Christ Himself, the great Head of the Church, has designed each local body. He has sovereignly designed that some be strong here and weak there, while others be weak here and strong there. And some see one doctrine clearly and another poorly; another, vice versa. So we need each other!

What is the Head of the Church saying to us? He's telling us not to despise His design of temporary inequality, but to see it as His Public School Number Seven, where we go to learn His grace.

We're not to get mad at each other.

We're to learn to "Be completely humble and gentle, [and to] be patient, bearing with one another in love" (Ephesians 4:2).

18
DON'T BE RUDE

Napoleon Bonaparte said, "I make servants; I never make friends."

He ended up on a Mediterranean island with neither servants nor friends. He died all alone.

Napoleon never understood that friends can bring out in us humility and grace. Having servants tends to make us proud.

We're apt to treat servants as things; you can get away with being rude to a servant. But God's Word says that "Pride goes before destruction, a haughty spirit before a fall" (Proverbs 16:18).

Personal ambition has brought many to ruin—and as a side effect destroyed many a friendship. Ambition uses people as servants—to get you from here to there, or to get you something you want. Servants can clean your house or do your laundry ... or they can get you connected to the right people or do a paperwork job you don't want to do.

In your own heart, how do you discourage rudeness and pride, and encourage humility and grace?

Join the servants!

Don't seek to be served, but to serve. This makes friends: Look to see where the servants are, and go hang out there!

A sure place to find friends is where the people in your church are serving. The level of your friendships kicks up a notch when you become a "fellow worker" with others who have pitched in to give themselves to the Lord's work. They're more apt to give themselves to you as well; they have that kind of heart.

The apostle Paul was rich in friendships; surely one reason was that so many of them were his "fellow workers."

He said his brother Apollos was his fellow worker (1 Corinthians 3:9).

He said twice that he and Timothy, his son in the Lord, were fellow workers (2 Corinthians 6:1; 1 Thessalonians 3:2).

He said two women, Euodia and Syntyche, as well as Clement and some others, were fellow workers (Philippians 4:2, 3).

He mentioned Aristarchus, John Mark, and Justus as among his Jewish fellow workers (Colossians 4:10, 11).

And in his very affectionate personal letter to Philemon, he called Philemon his "dear friend and fellow worker," and later said that they were "partners," using the word for deep fellowship, "koinonia" (Philemon 1, 17).

When you serve Christ with others, your very best friendships may be formed.

We were in a small group together a while back with a neat couple. We liked them a lot. But when they suggested our taking on an extra spiritual project with them, it certainly bumped our friendship up to a new level: we not only worked hard putting the project together and functioning in our weekly small group, but over the years we've had many a vacation together and loved each other well.

The Board of Directors of our Renewal Ministries, working with us these twenty years, has provided some of our closest friends: our dear Peggy and Jim (Jim now in heaven); Betty and Dick, our beloved neighbors in Pasadena whom we led to the Lord; our wonderful Bruce and Adaline (Forty-two years ago Bruce was the delegate on Lake Avenue Church's pastor search committee who flew to New York State to check us out and then recommended Ray to the committee).

Only the Lord knows how many hours we three couples have spent together the last quarter of a century—in Bible Study, in prayer for each other, in working through finances and reports, and much more. Now a couple in their thirties and another in their forties are joining our Board: Paul and Lisa and Greg and Stacey have not only been in our discipling groups but they've worked hard with us in other Christian projects.

And when we speak of fellow workers, of course, we list unbelievably faithful, loving Melinda. If serving the Lord the most and the hardest makes the friendship the deepest, Melinda qualifies. Only in her mid-forties, she's been with us in our Renewal Ministries office almost twenty years, and there's almost nothing she hasn't done. She arranges the traveling for our conferences and ships our books. She handles the finances. She word processes our new book manuscripts. She oversees all the mailings, including our Christmas cards. She plays taxi to and from the airport, even in off hours.

But more. She prays with us. She discusses theology with us. She weeps with us when we weep and rejoices when we rejoice. She enters into our lives so totally that she knows us better, almost, than we know ourselves. We found her wonderful husband John for her, and they named their daughter Rachel *Ray*.

Other people have seen her gifts and have offered her twice the salary—but we're together.

We're fellow workers.

Fellow workers don't tend to be rude to each other. They've voluntarily taken Jesus' yoke upon their shoulders together. They're learning of Him, and discovering that He is gentle and humble in heart, and in even their work they find rest for their souls (Matthew 11:29).

And it makes them love each other as dear friends.

Yes, Melinda and John.

19
DON'T BE SELF-SEEKING

Threesomes and foursomes of friends are very special and not easy to find. The dynamics are such that each of the group must respect each of the others as more or less equal. A big invisible sign hangs over them: "NO COMPETITION ALLOWED."

Each of the two of us Ortlunds has some separate very special friends of our own sex; mostly they're local people with whom we "do lunches," maybe even a sandwich on the beach. Then there are just a few couples who are special friends to us as a couple; with them the balance has to be just right. As foursomes or more we go to special church gatherings and plays and concerts and dinners. We do the same things as a threesome with single friends.

Threesomes and foursomes of friends in the Bible are just as rare and special. You have:

Paul, Silas, and Timothy traveling together in ministry (Acts 15:40-16:3).
Luke joining them for a foursome (Acts 16:10ff).
Paul joining a couple, Priscilla and Aquila (Acts 18:18ff).
And "the Glorious Company of the Stretcher-bearers," four who are unnamed friends in Mark 2:3-5. (Remember, they carried a paralytic to Jesus.)

Of this last group, a fellow of one of our small groups said, "I'd never have the courage to be the first guy to pick up the stretcher, but I'd be number four! I love to get close to guys like that and let it rub off on me." Not envy, but admiration.

There's a foursome in the book of Daniel exactly like that. Daniel seems to be the courageous leader, but the three others loved to follow and get in on the action.

(If you're feeling timid, buddy up to somebody with a special dose of courage. If you have rough edges, move close to someone sensitive and gentle. If you are overaggressive, make friends with a person known for restraint and wisdom—and so on. Rather than being envious, let iron sharpen iron, according to Proverbs 27:17.)

Daniel and his three friends were all of nobility, part of Judah's royal family—but Babylonians had conquered Judah and carried off anybody of value to their own land.

The king wanted to make the best of these useful to himself, so he ordered three years of special training for these four and others like them who were "Young men without any physical defect, handsome, showing aptitude for every kind of learning, well informed, quick to understand, and qualified to serve in the king's palace" (Daniel 1:4).

Daniel and his friends had no doubt known each other well back home as members of Judah's ruling class, but now they're especially thrown together to study the language and literature of the Babylonians.

Right off, the chief official gave them new names. It was part of a plan to brainwash out of them their former ways, including their former religion. Hebrews' names were always chosen in some way to honor God. Daniel's name, for instance, meant "My God is judge." His new name, Belteshazzar, meant "Bal [their god] protects his life"!

Maybe this obvious ploy even stiffened the resolve of these

four and bound their hearts together in a deeper relationship. Their names might be changed; their faith, never. And sure enough, the old names of Daniel's three friends are used in the first part of the book, but after that the text shifts over to what they were always called in their new life: Shadrach, Meshach, and Abednego.

Next, the chief official gave them a new diet, food that had first been offered to Babylon's pagan gods. The idea was that the spirit of the gods was passed into the food they ate, so that they would live by taking those pagan gods into their bodies.

At this idea, Daniel stepped forward as spokesman of the four.

Daniel said no.

They couldn't help their names, but they could help what they ate.

The chief official said yes:

"The king would have my head because of you" (1:10).

In a standoff, what does a foursome do? You don't blow your unity; you don't put yourself first; you don't get into envy and strife. You stand together. We think these three young friends did for Daniel what Jonathan did for his friend David—they "helped him find strength in God" (1 Samuel 23:16).

Daniel negotiated. "Give us ten days of plain food and water and see what happens."

Don't think for a minute this was some test of vitamins and minerals; no diet could change the four men's appearances in ten short days.

These were four men bound together in godly friendship,

refusing sin and prayerfully trusting God, by miracle, to save their lives as they obeyed Him.

And God did His miracle: "At the end of ten days they looked healthier and better nourished" (1:15), and He saved them.

Crisis over, they continued their training with the Lord's gracious blessing on their four heads: "To these four young men God gave knowledge and understanding of all kinds of literature and learning. And Daniel could understand visions and dreams of all kinds" (1:17).

Imagine their exciting fellowship and growing confidence together! They were a "God Squad" in Babylon. Yahoo! They might not have stood alone, but they had stood together. Result: "At the end of the time ... the king talked with them, and he found none equal to Daniel [and his friends.] So they entered the king's service" (1:19).

Next, Daniel interprets a dream for the king and is rewarded by being made ruler over the entire province of Babylon, and lavished with many gifts. So now he is truly a Big Shot; will he think of himself only?

At Daniel's request the king appointed Shadrach, Meshach and Abednego administrators over the province of Babylon, while Daniel himself remained at the royal court (2:49).

Now they're separated. The three are out in that pagan world, and they're in the public eye. Will they start to get political? Will they seek their own self-interests? Will they compromise the faith of their fathers?

The king erects a fabulous golden image of himself and

orders everybody in the kingdom, whenever they hear certain music, to fall down and worship it.

Shadrach, Meshach, and Abednego, to a man, say no.

Yea, guys!

Daniel must certainly have been somewhere praying for them.

For their refusal the three are thrown into a blazing furnace, heated seven times hotter than usual just for them—and the threesome becomes a foursome! The king cried, "Look! I see four men walking around in the fire, unbound and unharmed, and the fourth looks like the son of the gods" (3:25).

And when these three friends came out there wasn't even a smell of fire on them (3:27).

Have you ever been in a threesome in prayer, or doing exploits for God, and suddenly you knew that by miracle and grace, He had joined you and you were four?

Oh, pray for this kind of friendships, a circle without envy or strife, not loving self first but God and each other.

20
DON'T BE EASILY ANGERED

Imagine a human being boldly saying to Almighty God, the Maker of heaven and earth and Lord over all, "Now show me Your glory" (Exodus 33:18)!

And imagine Almighty God, whom "no one has ever seen" (John 1:18), being so softhearted toward the asker, His friend Moses, that He replies, "When my glory passes by, I will put you in the cleft of the rock and cover you with my hand until I have passed by. Then I will remove my hand and you will see my back; but my face must not be seen" (Exodus 33:22, 23).

When Moses was allowed to see God's backside, what did he see? He "saw" God's proclamation of who He is in relation to the people on His planet Earth. He saw that God is "The Lord,... compassionate, gracious, slow to anger ...," and other things.

It was a trembling peek into heaven, a fearful squint at the Person of God Himself, never to be forgotten. Eight more times in the Old Testament other writers repeated what God had told Moses He is like.

For one thing, He said He is "slow to anger."

God can get angry ("He does not leave the guilty unpunished," He said), but He is slow about it.

First Corinthians 13:5 says that's how love is. It doesn't say love never gets angry—there certainly is such a thing as righteous anger—but you don't rush into it. And you stay away from others who do.

Do not make friends with a hot-tempered man, do not
associate with one easily angered, or you may learn his
ways and get yourself ensnared.

PROVERBS 22:24, 25

[Ray writing] *One snowy day in Upper State New York,
Anne and I were arguing as we drove into our neighborhood,
going home. I blew my top, and in frustration turned the car
and drove it right into a snowbank. And along came our non-
Christian neighbor, to whom I'd been witnessing, who said,
"Ray! What are you doing in there?"!*

The story of Paul and Barnabas shows what hasty anger
can do to a friendship.

Barnabas, a generous-hearted fellow, loved giving people
the benefit of the doubt. (His name means "Son of
Encouragement.") Along comes a famous new convert Saul,
former persecutor of Christians, and nobody will take him in
except Barnabas, who takes his word for it that he's really
changed. But in the end Saul is labeled too controversial and
sent back to Tarsus, his hometown (Acts 9:20-30).

Time passes. Barnabas' ministry grows. He's so successful
at the church in Antioch that he needs help, and he remem-
bers Saul and sends for him. "So for a whole year Barnabas
and Saul met with the church and taught great numbers of
people. The disciples were called Christians first at Antioch"
(Acts 11:26).

What a happy team! Soon the Antioch church commissions
them to go on a ministry trip, and they take along a promis-
ing young fellow, John Mark (Acts 13:1-5).

John Mark was advantaged, both materially and spiritually.

Peter had apparently led him to Christ (1 Peter 5:13), and Barnabas was his cousin (Colossians 4:10). His mother Mary opened her large home to God's people (Acts 12:12, 13). He was probably a young favorite among the believers.

So off he goes with the "heavies." Saul (his name gets changed to Paul) is a hard driver. Paul takes over the leadership: first the team is "Barnabas and Saul," then it's "Paul and Barnabas," then it's "Paul and his companions." Young Mark is probably bugged that his cousin Barnabas has gotten muscled out of prominence. And there's the whirlwind schedule. Irregular meals. Little sleep.

Midstream, John Mark says "heck with it all" and goes back home to Mother.

Did tensions with young Mark, and then a lot of extra work when he deserted them, cool off Paul and Barnabas' relationship? They were both faithful, fervent men who went right on with their ministry trip—but did Paul talk harshly of Mark, while it was the very nature of Barnabas to get defensive and stand up for his young cousin?

All of us who've raised kids know how the tensions of disciplining get to a married couple, don't they! One wants to be tough when the other wants to be tender. We can understand how it might have been with those two coworkers.

Paul and Barnabas get home. They report in to the church. They get busy in the local work again (Acts 14:26-28).

But Barnabas, "Son of Encouragement," longs to redeem John Mark. It stays in his mind.

Paul's memories of the trip's tensions fade. After all, Barnabas is really a wonderful worker. It could be good a second time.

"Barnabas," he says, "let's go see how all the brothers are doing in the towns where we preached."

"Great," says Barnabas. "And let's give John Mark another chance."

Those smoldering coals of Paul's old anger immediately burst into flame! "Are you totally out of your mind?" And the fire in his heart raged.

"They had such a sharp disagreement that they parted company. Barnabas took Mark and sailed for Cyprus, but Paul chose Silas and ... went through Syria and Celicia...." (Acts 15:38-41).

It was a terrible thing.

Let's not ever glibly say, "Well, God loves ministry, and now there are two teams instead of one." That's like saying, "Divorce and remarriage are okay, because God loves families, and that makes two or three families where there was one."

It's true our sovereign Lord can cause the wrath of man ultimately to praise Him, but—

My dear brothers, take note of this: Everyone should be quick to listen, slow to speak and slow to become angry, for man's anger does not bring about the righteous life that God desires.

JAMES 1:19, 20

Paul is the favored one over Barnabas: Paul goes out on his second trip "commended by the brothers to the grace of the Lord" (Acts 15:40), while Barnabas is never heard of again.

But Paul's heart grieves. He may still feel his judgment was right, but his anger was wrong. Now he's been harsh not at one but at two, and both brothers in Christ. Anger is a bummer.

With more passage of time—we don't know how long—Paul is reconciled to young Mark, who has matured into a true man of God. Wherever Barnabas has gone, Mark can handle it; he has better perspective now; and he is loving and loyal to Paul.

In chains, Paul writes to the Colossians,

> My fellow prisoner Aristarchus sends you his greetings, as does Mark, the cousin of Barnabas. (You have received instructions about him [in other words, you know he's no longer considered a renegade but he's in full standing now]; if he comes to you, welcome him.)
>
> COLOSSIANS 1:10, brackets ours

And in Paul's last letter, written to Timothy before Paul's apparent indictment and execution, he writes, "Everyone but Luke has deserted me. Timothy, do your best to come to me quickly.... Get Mark and bring him with you, because he is helpful to me in my ministry" (2 Timothy 4:9, 11).

Paul was killed—but he had dealt with his anger.

It had left a scar, a bitter memory, a discredited believer. But his repenting of his anger and his relenting in his judgment of Mark, in the end accomplished what was in the heart of generous Barnabas—to encourage John Mark to become a great servant of God.

And even to become a writer of Holy Scripture, of the shortest and one of the most treasured of the Gospels.

21
KEEP NO RECORD OF WRONGS

Are you having trouble being a friend of your mother-in-law?

Something can turn sour in a mother's heart when some unworthy jerk goes off with her "baby." It's like being forced to put your Stradivarius violin into the hands of an 800-pound gorilla! For years after the wedding, her words and actions can reinforce the reputation of the "typical mother-in-law"—and in the minds of the married kids there's a growing record of wrongs.

How do you erase the record? How do you build a bridge? How do you become true friends with a mother-in-law?

You out-nice her.

Ruth tells you how to do it. Her story is a book of the Old Testament.

There's no record that Ruth was any beauty, like Sarah or Rebekah or Esther. She wasn't even young, like Rachel: her story begins when she'd been married about ten years and then was widowed. Ten years is a long time to build up her mother-in-law Naomi's record of wrongs.

Naomi was a bitter woman. She didn't even like her name, which meant "pleasant;" she preferred "Mara," which meant "bitter."

She and her husband didn't trust God when their area of Judah had a famine, so they took their two sons and moved to Moab, a wicked place and off-limits for Hebrews. She was a negative influence on those around her (Ruth 1:8-15). When her husband and both sons died she blamed God (Ruth 1:20, 21). And her ten years of bitterness so changed her looks that when she went home to live again, her old friends didn't recognize her (1:19).

But Ruth hadn't kept any record of Naomi's wrongs. She wasn't very beautiful, she wasn't very young, but she was *nice*.

When Naomi made up her mind to go back home, she thought she'd send her two Moabite daughters-in-law back to their pagan origins and just go it alone.

Ruth's speech to her in response is the speech of someone determined to be nothing less than a best friend:

She wanted shared experiences: "Where you go I will go."

She wanted shared responsibilities: "Where you stay I will stay."

She wanted shared relationships with Naomi's family and friends: "Your people will be my people."

She wanted shared spiritual commitment and growth: "Your God will be my God."

In fact, she wanted nothing less than a lifelong, unconditional commitment: "Where you die I will die, and there will I be buried" (Ruth 1:16, 17).

Loving the unlovely (as Ruth loved Naomi) is God-like: "God demonstrates his own love for us in this: While we were still sinners, Christ died for us" (Romans 5:8).

God Himself had given Ruth this kind of love for her mother-in-law. He knew the end of the story, that Ruth and her second husband Boaz would produce a baby son who would be the grandfather of King David, and in the family tree of Jesus Christ!

Ruth didn't know all this, and her challenges continued. Naomi reluctantly let her tag along back to Bethlehem, Naomi's hometown. And Naomi told her old friends, "Call me

Mara, because the Almighty has made my life very bitter. I went away full, but the Lord has brought me back empty" (1:20).

"Empty"? Ruth was standing right there beside her! To Naomi, Ruth was a nothing.

But Ruth out-niced her. Because there was no man in this new arrangement to provide for these two widows, Ruth volunteered to be the breadwinner for both of them.

She went out in the fields the way poor people did, picking up the leftover grain, and the foreman noticed how diligent she was: "She has worked steadily from morning until now, except for one short rest" (2:7).

And when Boaz the owner fed her lunch she only ate half, and took the rest home to Naomi, along with her day's work of sheaves of barley (2:18).

Notice, too, when Naomi gave Ruth instructions, her answer was, "I will do whatever you say" (3:5).

She just kept *out-nicing* her mother-in-law!

Gradually Naomi warmed up—and you know the story: Boaz the wealthy boss fell in love with nice Ruth, they married and had a baby boy.

By then all Naomi's friends were reminding her of several things: "Your daughter-in-law loves you" and "She's been better to you than seven sons" (4:15), the sons who normally would have taken care of her.

And Naomi took baby Obed on her knees, which was a symbol of adoption, and all the women crowed, "Naomi has a son!" (4:17).

And *Ruth had kept no record of Naomi's wrongs*, and mother-in-law and daughter-in-law lived happily ever after.

22

DON'T DELIGHT IN EVIL BUT IN TRUTH

There's a great difference between groups of friends who gather just to "hang out" and those who gather around the Lord. Haven't you noticed? Horizontal friendships are without direction, without purpose—without *Him*. And they easily degenerate into gossip ("slander, along with every form of malice," Ephesians 4:31), dirty jokes ("obscenity, foolish talk or coarse joking, which are out of place," Ephesians 5:4), and grumbling against authorities ("bitterness, rage and anger," Ephesians 4:31).

And they get a kick out of all that! They "delight in evil."

"But if we walk in the light, as he is in the light, we have fellowship with one another, and the blood of Jesus, his Son, purifies us from all sin" (1 John 1:7).

We open up our hearts to truth with each other. We let each other know what's inside of us—our joys, our hopes, our frustrations, our weaknesses, our sins, our triumphs—and the truth sets us free.

There's great comfort in being truly known—mars, scars, and all—and being accepted anyway. And the Lord commands it: "Accept one another, then, just as Christ accepted you, in order to bring praise to God" (Romans 15:7).

Phonies can't stand reality. But real friends push through the pain barriers of unpleasant surprises and inconsistencies and hurts to the place where they accept and are accepted. They "carry each other's burdens, and in this way [they] fulfill the law of Christ" (Galatians 6:2).

Someone has written,

Oh, the comfort, the inexpressible comfort, of feeling safe with a person, having neither to weigh thoughts nor measure words, but pour them all right out just as they are—chaff and grain together, knowing that a faithful hand will take and sift them, keep what is worth keeping and then, with the breath of kindness, blow the rest away.

Or, as one wise woman used to tell us, "Eat the chicken and spit out the bones."

Every year from September to June the two of us have small groups of disciples, five guys and five girls each; they're usually less than half our age. We pour into them not only Bible teaching but ourselves, the business of our hearts: what's happening in our lives and what we're struggling with and what we're happy about; they do the same.

We want to be like Paul, in his relationships with younger believers: "We loved you so much that we were delighted to share with you not only the gospel of God but our lives as well, because you had become dear to us" (1 Thessalonians 2:8).

In our groups we keep notebooks. Each of us has a page for each person in the group, and when we're sharing our lives together we jot the date under that person's name and take notes on what's going on. Obviously these are for faithful intercessory prayer.

We two have just gotten out old notebooks, and these were some past sharings of different people:

"Sept. 25: Pregnant! Sick! Pray for trip; I've often miscarried."

"Feb. 4: Pray for father-in-law and his third wife. They seem to resent our married joy."

"April 23: Two-week trip to London with wife. Pray for competent baby-sitter."

"Oct. 12: My manager [at dry-cleaning plant] has pneumonia. Should plant close briefly? I drive the truck, can't take her place. She's key to everything."

"Mar. 9: Feeling extra busy, uptight. Crabby at home."

"Jan. 22: "Interviewing for possible business partner. Pray for Christian."

"May 19: Pray for neighbors Frank, Pat, to meet the Lord."

"Oct. 19: Son Jeff defensive, resisting."

"Dec. 12: Great wedding anniversary!"

"Feb. 12: Hold me accountable for daily quiet times. Phone me, ask me."

We don't know any better way to know the hearts of a few other believers for loving encouragement and prayer than to meet with four to six of them weekly in a small group. For us, it's indispensable.*

One of the best small groups the two of us have been in together was four other couples and us. Early on, one of the wives said, "Couldn't we also have some kind of outreach meetings? I'm concerned about my own brother, and we all have friends who need the gospel."

So we decided to meet as our own support group three Thursday nights a month, and the fourth Thursday night

*For "how to's" on small groups see Anne's book, *Love Me with Stubborn Love* (Lincoln, Neb.: iUniverse.com, 2000).

we'd invite all the unbelievers we could for a hang-loose, discussion-type evangelistic Bible study.

We called it "Probe," because the purpose was to probe the Bible. The only format was to dig around together in a passage of Scripture and try to see what it said. Maybe twenty-five or thirty would gather in a neighborhood home for coffee and dessert, and then we'd discuss a passage we'd picked ahead of time. We led the thing really casually, and the Probers had no idea that there was a core group meeting the other Thursdays and praying for each of them by name!

That first night of Probe we'd phoned a ton of people and had dessert ready for a crowd. One guy showed up! It was that brother of the wife who had instigated it all. He knew the rest of us couples, and he backed against one of the walls and wisecracked, "You mean I'm the only sinner here??!" But that night, in front of us all, he took Christ to be his Savior! It was wonderful.

After that, bunches began to attend. One young divorcee said she could hardly wait now to get home from work each day and settle down with a cocktail and her new Bible.... During one of our closing prayer times a big-time executive alcoholic jumped to his feet and said, "God, Sir, I want to be a Christian!" Everybody yelled and applauded, and he went across the room and kissed his wife. (The wife accepted Christ a month later.)

God's hand was upon Probe, and the gospel became powerful in their eyes. Many received the Lord, right in front of the others. One housewife who was converted, from then on took it upon herself to challenge the others: "Hey, last month I did it. See, that's what you get for missing the meeting—you missed all the fireworks. So when are you going to do it? What are you waiting for? Hey, a car might run over you tomorrow, how do you know? Get with the program!" And many did.

After a few years we two moved away. But we had learned forever the power of groups who meet around the truth.

23

ALWAYS PROTECT

"She makes me feel as if I were bathed in sunshine," said Michelle to us about her Christian friend. Michelle knows that her friend is close enough to see plenty of her faults, but she also has the ingrained habit of protecting others, of "covering their backsides."

A friend knows the sins and weaknesses of the other but he doesn't advertise them; he leaves them unsaid.

"Blessed are the merciful" (Matthew 5:7).

It's God-like to protect: God loves to protect us.

Have you noticed how often the Bible realistically exposes a specific person's sins, but later on, from God's gracious perspective, mercifully deletes them? If that person has come under God's provision of atonement—well, God has promised us all, "I will remember their sins no more" (Jeremiah 31:34).

Levi was a bloody killer (Genesis 34:25), whose priestly tribe more than once led Israel into idolatry (Exodus 32:4). But God's atoning cover of blood (Leviticus 17:11) was so sufficient that in retrospect God describes Levi and his tribe like this: "He revered me and stood in awe of my name. True instruction was in his mouth.... He walked with me in peace and uprightness and turned away from sin" (Malachi 2:5, 6).

Lot made a bad choice in settling down in wicked Sodom (Genesis 13:10-13), and as the result lived a horrible life (Genesis 19). But in the New Testament God had the last word on how He saw Lot: "That righteous man, living among them day after day, was tormented in his righteous soul by the lawless deeds he saw and heard" (2 Peter 2:8).

Nevertheless, "[The Lord] is a shield to those who take refuge in him" (Proverbs 30:5).

Here are eight things God has done with all our ugly, embarrassing sins:

1. He has blotted them out (Isaiah 43:25).
2. He has swept them away like a cloud (Isaiah 44:22).
3. He has removed them from us as far as the east is from the west (Psalm 103:12).
4. He has put them all behind His back (Isaiah 37:17).
5. He has trodden them underfoot (Micah 7:19).
6. He has hurled them all into the depths of the sea (Micah 7:19).
7. He has forgiven them all (Colossians 2:13).
8. And He will remember them no more (Jeremiah 31:34; 50:20).

So about the believers all around you, who sin when they know it, who sin when they don't know it, who stumble and are miserable over it and dream of doing better ...

Give 'em some slack.

"You can always tell a real friend: when you've made a fool of yourself he doesn't feel you've done a permanent job."*

Ask the Lord for a sympathetic kindliness, a sweetness of temperament that puts others at ease and tries not to give pain.

"The lips of the righteous know what is fitting" (Proverbs 10:32).

---

*Lawrence J. Peter, *Peter's Quotes* (New York: Bantam, 1979).

"The tongue of the wise brings healing" (Proverbs 12:18).

So wrap yourself, like putting on your clothes, with "compassion, kindness, humility, gentleness and patience" (Colossians 3:12). Your lovingness will be what you wear, and it will produce its own atmosphere everywhere you go.

Above all, love each other deeply, because love covers over a multitude of sins.

1 PETER 4:8

[Ray writing] *Peter and I were just acquaintances until he went through a severe marriage crisis. I had the privilege of standing by him and his wife, and over time watching God make him a man of God, and his wife, a gracious and loving partner.*

Since then, a couple of decades now, Peter and I have been friends. At first the ups and downs he would tell me about were just his, and the ups and downs I would tell him about were just mine; but now all our ups and downs belong to each other. Our friendship has grown deeper than either of us planned it to be. We've shared our souls, and then looked together to the One who gives true understanding and peace.

We don't schedule these "brother times." Pete just picks up the phone and says, "Rev, I think you need me to straighten you out again. How about lunch?" We go get a sandwich and sit on a bench at the beach, and God moves in close.

I love that man, and he loves me. It doesn't get any better than this.

And then, not only cover your friend's faults—forget them

all, past, present, and future!—but also exaggerate and delight in all his possible pluses! Crow over them! Enjoy them out of all realistic proportion, because he's your buddy.

Norma used to be the receptionist at the offices of the Haven broadcast, and she had that way of delighting in other people.

When Norma died a huge crowd showed up at her memorial service. There was a time of sharing, and one of those in the crowd who stood up said, "I was Norma's best friend."

When she finished the next person to speak said, "I always thought *I* was Norma's best friend."

Then several others who stood up each said, "I'm so surprised; I really thought *I* was her best friend!"

And the rest of us laughed, because we all had somewhat the same feeling.

There is something wonderful about supporting and delighting in your friends. We think of Armin and Reidun, Carol, Saskia, Joel and Kay, and Bill and Deanne, who do that. They're all cheerleaders!

Our dear friend Marie was talking to her husband Clare, who's in the middle stage of Alzheimer's disease. He still recognizes her, and for companionship and comfort she talks to him.

She told us recently she happened to remark to him, "Oh, if I could live my life over, there are so many things I'd change."

In a sudden, brief moment of lucidity, Clare answered in clear words, "A shovel can't dig the same hole twice."

To Marie it was like parents' seeing their baby's first step, for the thrill of it, the delight, the wonder. She loves telling people about it.

24
ALWAYS TRUST

Start giving your friends the benefit of the doubt.

Of course it's a challenge to learn to trust them—the possibility exists that later on they'll let you down.

But what's the alternative? If your habit is not to trust them, you become a suspicious, doubting, pessimistic, worrying, cynical kind of person. Is that what you want?

Pat hated Mike because every time Mike talked to him he thumped him on the chest. Pat's chest was actually sore from all Mike's thumpings. So one day Pat got a stick of dynamite and strapped it to his chest under his shirt. "Now," he said, "the next time my friend Mike thumps my chest...."

As we said, how you react may hurt yourself, too.

In the early centuries of the British Isles, those inhabitants used words which are still in use in our English language: for instance, the word "fee." We talk about a doctor's fee or a lawyer's fee; it has to do with money.

In those early British days there was no actual money—no bills or coins—and the people's cows, which they called their "fees," were what they often used for currency. If you wanted to sell your house you set the price at so many fees, or cows.

Suppose a man had a rather small herd of fees and he saw that his neighbor's herd was also rather small; he might think to himself, "Why should we pay the salaries of two men to look after our fees when one would do?"

So the neighbors might decide to trust each other, and they'd tear down the fence between their properties and put their fees all together. And they called that "fee-lowship," and so the word was coined. We're told that's a true bit of history.

The basic idea behind fellowship is still trust, and 1 Corinthians 13:7 says that love "always trusts."

That's what makes fellowship strong and durable.

That's what makes good friendships possible.

When you hear negative things said about your friend, *decide to trust him.* Make up your mind that he's innocent until proven guilty.

"He who seeks good finds good will" (Proverbs 11:27).
   He always trusts.
"He who covers over an offense promotes love" (Proverbs 17:9).
   He always trusts.
"He who loves a pure heart and whose speech is gracious
      will have the king for his friend" (Proverbs 22:11).
   He always trusts.
"A man's wisdom gives him patience; it is to his glory to
      overlook an offense" (Proverbs 19:11).
   He always trusts.
"A friend loves at all times" (Proverbs 17:17).
   He always trusts.

25

ALWAYS HOPE

What happens when your good friend comes into bad times?

A friend loves at all times, and a brother is born for adversity.

PROVERBS 17:17

Notice he wasn't born for his own adversity, but for his friend's.

Sometimes friends can be friends a long time, and then something terrible happens to one of them. For the other, the moment of reality has come.

Mordecai challenged his cousin Queen Esther, when their fellow Jews fell into a trauma, "Who knows but that you have come to royal position for such a time as this?" (Esther 4:14).

Consider the possibility that you, too, were born for such a time as this—that your friend's adversity will bring you into your finest hours.

We know two women, one married and one single, who have been friends for maybe half a century. For probably the past thirty-five years, the single gal has gone in and out of severe depression. When she's well, the two go shopping or have meals or go to church together. When the single one is raging, either at home or in the hospital, her friend just as faithfully takes her meals or gifts or simply visits her. The friendship goes on unabated.

Two other friends of ours have been married for a long

time—all their adult lives—and now she's just been diagnosed with early Alzheimer's disease. The husband looked us straight in the eye recently, understanding what's coming, and said, "When we got married I signed up for this, or for anything else."

Married friends, hear these words again:

> For better or for worse,
> For richer or for poorer,
> In sickness and in health,
> As long as we both shall live.

This isn't a trap. Whatever comes from your Father's wise and loving hand, "May the God of hope fill you with all joy and peace as you trust in him, so that you may overflow with hope by the power of the Holy Spirit" (Romans 15:13).

He may choose to reverse the situation. In any case—whatever comes, it's to usher you into your finest hours of growth and grace.

It's to bring you into "royal position for such a time as this."

26

ALWAYS PERSEVERE

[Anne writing] My friend Debbie is in her forties, and I've known her since before she started first grade. When I was the pastor's wife and she was Little Miss Twinkle Toes with bobbing black curls and patent leather Mary Jane shoes, we didn't have a lot in common; I knew her parents better. But thirteen years ago Debbie was in my small group and we got close. In fact, that year all the group went over to her house the week before she married Rob, and we ooh'd and ah'd over her gorgeous wedding dress.

The next year her good friend Joy was in a mixed group with Ray and me. Beautiful blond Joy was in love with Will, and all of us, married or single, fervently prayed all year for God to put those two wonderful people together.

Today Debbie and Joy and I had lunch together, as we have periodically these thirteen years. Debbie is Rob's wife, Joy is Will's wife, and their children played together outside while we ate.

I had just yesterday read Malachi 3:16, and that verse tells just what the three of us love to do:

Then those who feared the Lord talked with each other, and the Lord listened and heard. A scroll of remembrance was written in his presence concerning those who feared the Lord and honored his name.

What a verse for dear friendships! And their friendship with me is a persevering one, even to the next generation: one of their daughters is named for me. They could well do without me but they refuse to, and I feel so rich. God's grace is upon them and upon me and upon our bond together.

There's a wonderful couple of men in the Old Testament with a persevering friendship: David and Jonathan.

Maybe when David wrote in one of his psalms, "As for the saints who are in the land, they are the glorious ones in whom is all my delight" (16:3), he was thinking especially of his best friend Jonathan.

David's friendship with this remarkable fellow was absolutely God-made, and at just the proper time God brought them together.

The Philistines were threatening to do Israel in; Israel's leader, King Saul, was weak and scared; his army was intimidated and morale was low. But then onto the scene step two soldiers, fearless in their confidence in God and ready to tackle the world.

One is Jonathan, King Saul's son and Crown Prince of Israel. He had already proven himself in small skirmishes (1 Samuel 14) and won the admiration of everyone.

The other is David, younger, unknown and untried. But when he dares to take on the enemy's champion, Goliath, he wins Jonathan's heart. Back comes David from the valley of battle with his little slingshot, and the huge head of Goliath in one hand and Goliath's sword in the other (1 Samuel 17).

And Prince Jonathan says, "That's my man!"—

Jonathan became one in spirit with David, and he loved him as himself.

1 Samuel 18:1

(*The Expositor's Bible* commentary says, "The word for 'love' in 1 Samuel 18:3 is not a sexual love. The Hebrew has another word altogether for that. This word defines being one in spirit. It has to do with an incredible unity, or being closely bound up in the life of another."*)

These two were brought together by God for his own purposes. Their friendship was His doing, His miracle.

Jonathan, above David in rank and age, usually took the lead in developing their relationship: "And Jonathan made a covenant with David because he loved him as himself. Jonathan took off the robe he was wearing and gave it to David, along with his tunic, and even his sword, his bow and his belt" (1 Samuel 18:3, 4).

David gained great symbols of royalty. Jonathan gained nothing but a friend. But Jonathan was saying, "David, all that I have is yours."

If your friend is really your friend, be willing to strip yourself of your valuables for him—your time, your money, your loving care, your loyalty, and more.

[Anne writing] When my dear friend and Pasadena neighbor Betty came to know the Lord, she was excited in her new life to obey everything the Scriptures said. One day she was reading Acts 4:32:

All the believers were one in heart and mind. No one claimed that any of his possessions was his own, but they shared everything they had.

*Vol. 3, page 707.

Betty's heart was so filled with love for me because I had led her to know Christ, that she called me across the street and gave me a number of her beautiful clothes. We wear the same size, and she picked out things (with her exquisite taste) that she thought would look good on me—and they did.

It was the beginning of a lifelong friendship, for which we made a particular covenant. Long after we had moved from Pasadena, Betty wrote me a letter repeating our covenant, which I always keep in my notebook:

"Dearest Anne, How blessed I am to call you sister and friend! How blessed I am that God chose you to transmit real life to me. How joyous that bonds in Him are forever. How neat to start a new year with these reflections and assurances.

"January, 1984— our covenant:

"We shall not get stale.

"We will stay childlike and awed.

"We will stay full of wonder over Jesus.

"We will stay eager to grow in Him.

"Yes! Yes! Yes!"

The word "covenant" in the Hebrew means "to cut." In biblical days, when men made a covenant with each other they actually made a small incision in their arms and sealed their covenant with their blood. A covenant was a serious thing, and they could expect it to involve suffering.

And so it happened with Jonathan and David. Jonathan's father King Saul was very jealous of David, as you remember, and David became a fugitive, always defending his life against Saul or his men. Still, Jonathan sought him out in his hiding places. In one instance Jonathan said to David, "Whatever you want me to do, I'll do for you" (1 Samuel 20:4). There was total trust.

And then there's the tender scene, during another rendezvous, when David "bowed down before Jonathan three times, with his face to the ground. Then they kissed each other and wept together—but David wept the most" (1 Samuel 20:41).

Now Jonathan added a new dimension to their pact; he said, "The Lord is witness between you and me and between your descendants and my descendants forever" (1 Samuel 20:42).

[Ray writing] *Once a dear friend said to me, after we'd had a wonderful time of prayer, "Ray, if I should die and you are still living, will you look after my wife and children?" I suppose there's no greater request than that.*

At another secret meeting Jonathan and David reconfirmed their covenant to each other (1 Samuel 23:15-18). Old promises often need renewing. Friendships in this world tend to deteriorate, and we need to continually express our love and commitment to a spouse or to a soul-buddy.

[Ray writing] *When Ed, my "Jonathan," and I meet, I often tell him how much I appreciate his friendship and our commitment to each other. We're very different, but that in itself enriches my life. I tell him I love him, and I often go home to Anne and say what a great brother in Christ he is to me.*

The sad end to David's friendship came when both Jonathan and King Saul were killed in battle. David was devastated. Weeping, he wrote, "How the mighty have fallen in battle! Jonathan lies slain on [Gilboa's] heights. I grieve for you, Jonathan my brother; you were very dear to me. Your love for me was wonderful, more wonderful than that of women. How the mighty have fallen!" (2 Samuel 1:25-27).

And David indeed became King of Israel, but he didn't forget his covenant with his friend. He asked, "Is there anyone still left of the house of Saul to whom I can show kindness for Jonathan's sake?" (2 Samuel 9:1).

He's told there's a son of Jonathan's crippled in both his feet. And David takes him in to be like one of his own sons, always eating at the king's table.

'Attaway, David!

Don't live the rest of your life without special and rare friendships! Be hungry for them! Maybe you'll even become a David to some Jonathan.

As you pray and seek who it should be, God will lead you to the right person or people.

As Nike says, *Just do it.*

27
THE FRIEND WHO NEVER FAILS: JESUS

There was nothing Pat wouldn't do for Mike, and there was nothing Mike wouldn't do for Pat. So they spent their whole lives doing nothing for each other.

After all we've said in this book; after all you've read in other wonderful books about friendships; even after all the Spirit of God has given in warnings, advice, and life illustrations in His Book—

Sometimes friendships just don't take off. Or they start off with hope but then they fizzle.

You've tried to follow the rules, you've prayed, still your relationship falters and dies. What can you say?

Don't stake your all on any human friend. Anything as frail as humanity sometimes collapses.

Dietrich Bonhoeffer says an interesting thing, that there must always be a little distance between the closest of humans; Christ must be between.*

"Close," humanly speaking, just may be too close.

If you find honey, eat just enough—
too much of it and you will vomit.

Seldom set foot in your neighbor's house—
too much of you and he will hate you.

PROVERBS 25:16, 17

*Dietrich Bonhoeffer, *Life Together* (New York: Harper Brothers, 1954), 32, 33.

Job, in his day, was God's finest specimen of a man, who should have been loved fervently; but poor Job mourned, "My friends have forgotten me" (Job 19:14).

Even the Lord Jesus, not long after He told His disciples "you are my friends," was forsaken by every one of them (Matthew 26:56).

Oh, how that had to hurt! Try to think how Jesus felt when Judas Iscariot actually betrayed Him—and with a kiss, at that! The destitute feelings of God Almighty, spurned by a man into whom He'd unstintingly poured His heart—those feelings had been recorded a thousand years before in two prophetic psalms:

> If an enemy were insulting me, I could endure it.... But it is you, a man like myself, my companion, my close friend, with whom I once enjoyed sweet fellowship."
>
> PSALM 55:12-14

And Psalm 41:9: "Even my close friend, whom I trusted, he who shared my bread, has lifted up his heel against me."

The sting of this, the excruciating pain.... A divorce can be an example of this kind of rejection; some of you reading this know it well.

And it hurts God more than it hurts us. The prophet Malachi, in pleading for unity, wrote, "Have we not all one Father? Did not one God create us? Why do we profane the covenant of our father by breaking faith with one another?" (Malachi 2:10).

We had two friends who really became "David and Jonathan" to each other. Steve, a mature Christian, was doing well in his medical practice. Chris, a new believer, was a dynamic witness for Christ and a sharp young businessman. These two grew to love each other, and they shared a dream. Steve put in his money and Chris gave his time and business know-how, and together they started a Christian enterprise which was needed and which did well.

Then what happened? What made things turn sour? Chris divorced his wife and turned to drugs. Steve held to the straight and narrow and broke with his friend—before the troubles? During the troubles? After the troubles? We don't know. Chris, a wonderful guy, is now back in fellowship again with the Lord; but the friendship, once such a blessing to so many onlookers including new Christians, is over.

So about friendships—don't be pessimistic, cynical, suspicious. When you find a good friend, expect the best. Still, don't possess him completely, don't overwhelm him, don't stake your all on him.

The Lord Jesus Christ, God Himself, is the only One who has said, "Surely I am with you always, to the very end of the age" (Matthew 28:20). "I will never leave you nor forsake you" (Joshua 1:5). And, "He who promised is faithful" (Hebrews 10:23).

No matter what, other humans let you down,

> For the weariest day
> May Christ be thy stay.
> For the darkest night
> May Christ be thy light.
> For the weakest hour

May Christ be thy power.
    For each moment's fall
May Christ be thy all.*

Tell this Best of all friends, "Lord, Thou hast made us for Thyself, and our hearts are restless until they rest in Thee."

Thee will I cherish,
Thee will I honor,
Thou, my soul's glory, joy and crown!**

---

*Old benediction.
*"Fairest Lord Jesus," 17th century hymn.

Epilogue

Adam, Where Are You?

"I have loved you," says the Lord.

MALACHI 1:2

"Yes, yes, I know that," many Christians answer carelessly.
"'Jesus-loves-me-this-I-know-for-the-Bible-tells-me-so.' I
grew up on that. Tell me something that's more of a grabber."

Someone has said, "We get to grace too fast."

Not many Christians read the Bible straight through, to get
a grasp of God's prolonged agony over so many centuries of
His people's continually turning away from Him. They "don't
get" the absolute wickedness, helplessness, lostness, and
hopelessness of our own condition without God. Or the inten-
sity of His passion to woo us back to Himself:

> "Place me like a seal over your heart [He says,] like a seal
> on your arm; for love is as strong as death, its jealousy
> unyielding as the grave. It burns like blazing fire, like a
> mighty flame. Many waters cannot quench love; rivers
> cannot wash it away. If one were to give all the wealth of
> his house for love, it would be utterly scorned."

SONG OF SOLOMON 8:6, 7

With this kind of love for you God the Son went to His
death, claiming, as well, the power of His resurrection, to
achieve for you true life in all its glory. Only His amazing
grace—"grace that is greater than all our sin"—dragged you
out of condemnation the way angels dragged Lot out of
Sodom when it was about to burn; and only His amazing
grace placed you as a seal upon His arm forever.

"'I have loved you,' says the Lord."

And he asks for your response.

A friendship is a two-way commitment. In 2 Corinthians 5:19, 20 God says, "I've already been reconciled to you. Now will you be reconciled to Me?"

> This is love: not that we loved God, but that he loved us and sent his Son as an atoning sacrifice for our sins.
>
> 1 JOHN 4:10

Because of the cross God is already your Friend; now will you be His friend?

Oh, this is wonderful—the opportunity of your lifetime— because what He has in mind is no casual, careless acquaintance. God doesn't want your being a Christian to be just your title, or just the activities you do; God wants it to become a precious, day-to-day, "I-thou" friendship with Himself.

So how do you respond?

He has only one stipulation. He says to you,

> My command is this: Love each other as I have loved you. Greater love has no one than this, that he lay down his life for his friends. You are my friends if you do what I command.
>
> JOHN 15:12-14

"If you do what I command." Well, He'd just told us His command—to love each other (verse 12.)* That's God's qualification, His only ground rule, if you want to return the friendship He offers you.

---

*Though the original "what" in verse 14 is plural, because of the proximity of verse 12 it is valid to interpret this as obedience to the command in verse 12 to love each other.

Do you see how crucial this command is, Christian, for your whole life—for your spiritual health, for your walk with God? Your own obedience in friendships with believers is the response He asks for.

Here's an important insight for your life. If you have problems loving fellow Christians, you're cutting yourself off from that friendship relationship with Jesus Christ which He's offering you. It doesn't mean you're not saved; it means you're cool toward Christ; you're stiff-arming Him. If you hold fellow believers at a distance, you hold Christ at a distance, too.

Saul was rushing around persecuting Christians when Jesus confronted him and said, "Saul, Saul, why do you persecute me?" (Acts 9:4). Saul thought he was only persecuting *Christians*—but if you hurt the Body the Head hurts, too.

Ephesians 4:31 says, "Get rid of all bitterness, rage and anger, brawling and slander, along with every form of malice." And the verse next to it says, "Do not grieve the Holy Spirit of God"—literally, "Don't make God cry."

We said it before: If you hurt the Body the Head hurts, too. Don't ever forget how closely connected the two are. *If you hold fellow believers at a distance, you hold Christ at a distance, too.*

So do you want to sign up for God's offer? Do you want to become His friend? Then "love each other." Reach out to your fellow Christians. Become friends with them, and you'll become a friend of Jesus.

The Scriptures tell you how to do it:

Comfort one another.
Edify one another.
Teach and admonish one another.
Bear with one another.
Don't lie to one another.
Greet one another with a holy kiss.
Care for one another.
Submit to one another.
Confess your faults to one another.
Serve one another.
In honor prefer one another.
Forgive one another.
Encourage one another.
Be kind to one another.
Love one another.

The Lord says to us, "I tell you the truth, whatever you did for one of the least of these brothers of mine, you did for me" (Matthew 25:40).

And He says, "Whatever you did not do for one of the least of these, you did not do for me" (Matthew 25:45).

The two of us have written this book to you, to urge you to get a fresh start—a fresh start in becoming a friend and in making friends.

This book is about the happy job of being friends with all the body of Christ, and then going deeper with a few.

And it's about discovering, then, that because you love each other, you've become a friend of Jesus Christ!

Christian, He offers you this.

The next step is up to you.

We'd be honored if you shared
your response with us.
Write to:
Ray and Anne Ortlund
4500 Campus Drive, Suite 662
Newport Beach, CA 92660